Historic Restaurants of BILLINGS

STELLA FONG

FOREWORD BY
GREG PATENT

AMERICAN PALATE

Published by American Palate
A Division of The History Press
Charleston, SC
www.historypress.net

Front cover, top, left to right: The Charles O. Myers home was converted to the Skyline Club in 1944. Later, it took on the name of the Bella Vista Club. *Courtesy of Stella Fong*; Waitresses at the Golden Belle in the Northern Hotel. Third from the right is Doris Waddell, late 1950s. *Courtesy of Karen Waddell.*

Front cover, bottom, left to right: The Elmo Club on Laurel Road around 1946. *Courtesy of James M. Reich*; Western Days in front of the Stockman Cafe, "The Reason I Forgot to Dress Western," 1940s. *Courtesy of the Western Heritage Center.*

Back cover, top to bottom: A postcard of the Northern Hotel, "the Largest and Finest Hotel in Montana," 1960s. *Courtesy of Billings Public Library*; Log Cabin Tavern, U.S. Cafe, St. Louis Cafe, Hotel Carlin and Billings Brewing Company on Montana Avenue, 1940s. *Courtesy of James M. Reich.*

First published 2015

Manufactured in the United States

ISBN 978.1.46711.758.6

Library of Congress Control Number: 2015948832

For my husband, Joe, who has created many delicious memories in my life

CONTENTS

CONTENTS

FOREWORD

Food is central to all our lives, and restaurants have consistently played an important role in defining who we are as a people. Stella Fong shows us how this happens in her highly entertaining historic and contemporary look at Billings' restaurants. The *Billings Herald* on November 23, 1882, reported: "Billings has always been singularly blessed in the matter of restaurants and a good meal is always obtainable at a fair price." Foods from far away such as oysters, salmon and European cured meats made their long trek west by ship and by train. Equidistant from St. Paul, Minnesota, and Seattle, Washington, Billings was the nascent commercial center to and from points west, north and south. And to serve the workers pouring into the area, lodging and restaurants became necessities.

Starting with the Fulton Market Restaurant and the Vienna Bakery in 1882 and moving on to the Northern Hotel, the Luzon Cafe, the Stockman and dining and dancing establishments, such as the Elmo Club, we learn about the fabulous entrepreneurs Henry W. Rowley and P.B. Moss, who built the original Northern Hotel in 1904, a favored destination for the traveler and social center for the city; Robert James "Bob" Porter, who had worked in the oil fields and in road construction and ultimately took over the fashionable Elmo Club and made it the hot spot for dining and dancing; and for that special western hospitality, Quincy A. Edwards, Frank J. Rogers and J.B. Webster, owners of the Stockman, a place "Where Men Meet Men."

Many other Billings eateries and clubs receive Stella's fond descriptions, and we learn of just about all the establishments that have been or still are servicing the city and its environs. Today, some of the original establishments still exist: the Northern Hotel on Broadway, rebuilt and relocated from its original location; Rex Restaurant Bar and Grill on Montana Avenue, the most famous and historic Billings steakhouse; and the Granary, another carnivore favorite.

As food trends across the nation evolved, Billings became home to a number of talented chefs. James Honaker, founder of the short-lived La Toque and the current Bistro Enzo, serves American, French, Italian and Asian cuisine in a European atmosphere. Carl Kurokawa, executive chef and proprietor of Juliano's Restaurant, offers American and European food with Asian influences. Bill Honaker and his brother, James, opened Walkers Grill in 1993 and based their menu on "New American Cooking" as practiced by Alice Waters of Chez Panisse in Berkeley, California. All these chefs source foods locally and seasonally.

And so it goes. Dozens more food establishments and clubs have shaped and continue to shape Billings' restaurant scene. May the long parade continue and flourish.

Greg Patent
James Beard Award–winning cookbook author for *Baking in America*
and thebakingwizard.com

ACKNOWLEDGEMENTS

I want to thank Joyce Jensen for her contagious enthusiasm and incredible historical knowledge. Many thanks to Kevin Kooistra, the historian at the Western Heritage Center (WHC), for providing invaluable information but, even more, for giving me new insight on how to view and appreciate the gifts of history. Also thanks to WHC volunteer and outreach coordinator Elisabeth DeGranier for research assistance.

I thank Greg Patent, who has been a mentor, supporter and friend from the culinary world. He has always led by example—sharing passion and hard work.

Many thanks to Cody Allen and Dee Ann Redman at the Billings Public Library for their guidance and support. I thank Mike Cruzan of Photographic Solutions and his Hunter for their patience and for capturing the images in this book.

I am thankful for the generosity and knowledge of Jim Reich for sharing his collection of images, menus, tableware and stories from Billings' historic restaurants.

The help Kathleen Garibay, P.J. Smith and Jennifer Hodges provided in research, editing and data organizing were tremendously appreciated. Many thanks to Deb Goffena for her always artistic eye. To Norma Buchanan, Mike Nelson, Lezlie Solari, Tom Nelson, Christine Twito, James Honaker, Steve Corning, Corby Skinner, Gene Burgad, Mike Schaer, Carl Kurokawa, Bill Honaker, Mike Callahan, Randy Holbrook, Lynda Moss, Rhonda Malloy, Chuck Hauptman, Mike Sammartino, Bess Fredlund, Kim Hauptman,

Pete Zagorda, Ying Lee Custer, Don Lee, Clint Peck, Susan Carlson, Karen Waddell, Kenny and Diane Roesch and Marie Halone, I am grateful for all your savory stories and remembrances.

I thank Mary Underriner, Margit Thorndal, Kari Knierim, Terrie Chrones, Barb Andersen and Jeanne Moller for their nurturing and cheer. Gratitude to Bernard Rose for his direct outlook and sage input. I extend gratitude to Robin Kline, my stalwart friend and food lover. Many thanks to Sean McDaniel and his wife, Tiki, for their advice and encouragement to write. I thank Renee Coppock for her confidence and calm and invaluable comments.

Mostly, I thank my husband, Joe Dillard, for his ceaseless support and for his belief in me.

Finally, many thanks to Artie Crisp of The History Press for his direction and guidance on this project. Also, I am tremendously grateful to Hilary Parrish from the editorial department for her eye for detail.

I thank many others for the delectable tales they shared of dining and celebrating in Magic City restaurants from yesteryear. These stories have added flavor to this book.

INTRODUCTION

In *Historic Restaurants of Billings*, I hope to share the flavor of the period when Billings was founded and establishing its culinary landscape. I endeavor to provide a sampling of the eateries and the entrepreneurs by covering the iconic and popular restaurants of the times. My research includes lesser-known pioneers, restaurants and bakeries to demonstrate the risks that were taken to share their passion for food. I interviewed current chefs who have attempted to alter the food scene and those business innovators who have changed the food landscape forever.

With the arrival of the railroad, tracks were laid for good food to come to Billings. The path was set to bring in the people and products to establish the restaurants that would feed, nourish and entertain hearty and diverse appetites. The population of Billings expanded rapidly, earning the nickname "Magic City." The magic allowed for limitless possibilities, but magic also implied that the opportunities might be hidden. Those who settled in the town, now rebranded as "Montana's Trailhead," were gifted with a landscape of opportunity for growth. These people learned to cherish and to work with what the city offered. These industrious settlers have left their mark on Billings, and their spirit still reigns.

I hope *Historic Restaurants of Billings* provides you with a good sampling of the establishments that brought deliciousness and nourishment to those who lived and those who passed through the Magic City.

1
IN THE BEGINNING

Looking Deliciously to Billings

In the 1800s, America looked deliciously toward the west. Railroad tracks provided the arteries for bringing life into new territories. Towns were born to serve the needs of the people creating the railway and then for those who arrived on the tracks once the towns were established. In these settlements, services emerged to provide for all the basic necessities, with the most rudimentary of requirements: food. With the presence of the tracks extending from afar, delicacies such as oysters and salmon, European cheeses and cured meats became obtainable and available.

In 1882, the city that was quickly becoming a center point for progress adopted the name of a Northern Pacific Railway president, Frederick H. Billings. The newly founded town, Billings, located on a section of the Yellowstone River Valley known as the Clark's Fork Bottom, was equidistant to St. Paul, Minnesota (about 850 miles, the boomtown of the times), and Seattle, Washington (820 miles, a future commercial center and resource). But according to Myrtle E. Cooper, author of *From Tent Town to City: A Chronological History of Billings, Montana 1882–1935*, "The Billings of 1882 exemplified the Old West in every respect. It was a land of dusty trail herds, leather-lunged bullwhackers, and bandy-legged cowpokes—a land of pioneers."

Billings established itself as the pivot point for commodities movement from the then established trade center of St. Paul on the Mississippi River to the new markets in the West and to directions north and south. In a communication to the *Chicago Interocean*, General James Brisbin nicknamed Billings the "Magic

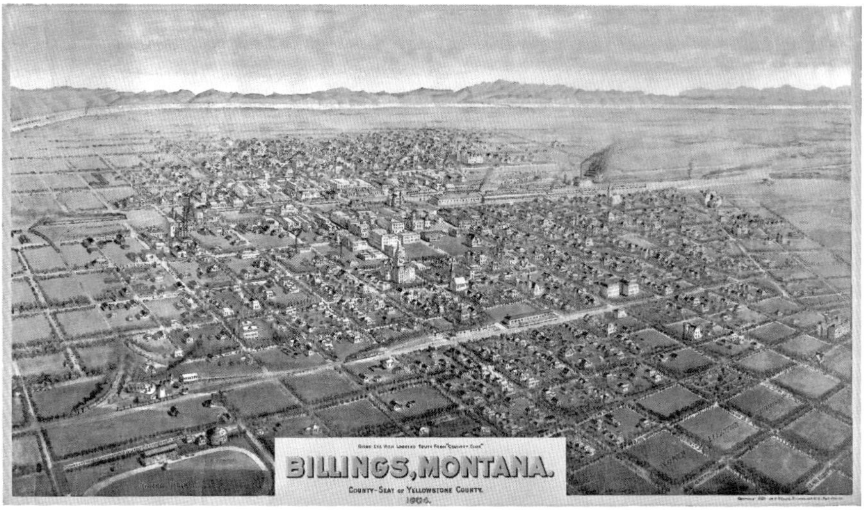

Above: A bird's-eye view of Billings in 1904. *Courtesy of Billings Public Library*.

Left: Peter Yegen opened P. Yegen and Co. on Minnesota Avenue and North Twenty-eighth Street with brother Christian in 1882. *Courtesy of Billings Public Library*.

City" of the plains because he believed "somewhere between the Mississippi River and the Rocky Mountains a great city is to grow."

Peter Yegen and his brother Christian opened a bakery and a small grocery store on Minnesota Avenue and Twenty-eighth Street, selling grocery staples and canned and baked products. The brothers, born in Switzerland, arrived in Billings in the spring of 1882 and, by the turn of the century, as advertised in the July 24, 1932 *Billings Gazette*, had expanded their first store to selling "hardware, implements, clothing, dry goods and every other essential to the well-being of Billings settlers. In a comparatively few years Yegen's policy of fair dealing made their store the greatest trading center in all eastern and southern Montana."

In the early summer of 1882, it was reported in the *Coulson-Billings Post* that "a newcomer is quoted as hearing in towns to the east that nothing could be had to eat in Billings." The editor of the paper rebutted the claim and proclaimed five new restaurants in the city, with two more opening soon.

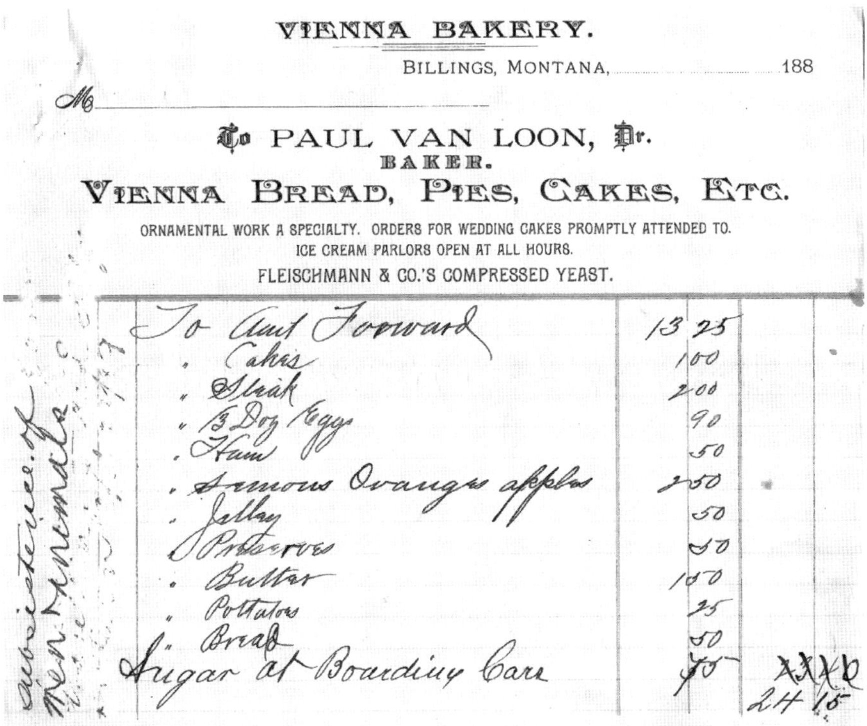

VIENNA BAKERY.

BILLINGS, MONTANA, ...188

M..........

To PAUL VAN LOON, Dr.

BAKER.

VIENNA BREAD, PIES, CAKES, ETC.

ORNAMENTAL WORK A SPECIALTY. ORDERS FOR WEDDING CAKES PROMPTLY ATTENDED TO.

ICE CREAM PARLORS OPEN AT ALL HOURS.

FLEISCHMANN & CO.'S COMPRESSED YEAST.

To Acct Forward	13 25	
" Cakes	1 00	
" Steak	2 00	
" 3 Doz Eggs	90	
" Ham	50	
" Lemons Oranges apples	2 50	
" Jelly	50	
" Preserves	50	
" Butter	1 50	
" Pottatoes	25	
" Bread	50	
" Sugar at Boarding Care	50	
		24 15

A receipt from the Vienna Bakery to Paul Van Loon, late 1800s. *Courtesy of James M. Reich.*

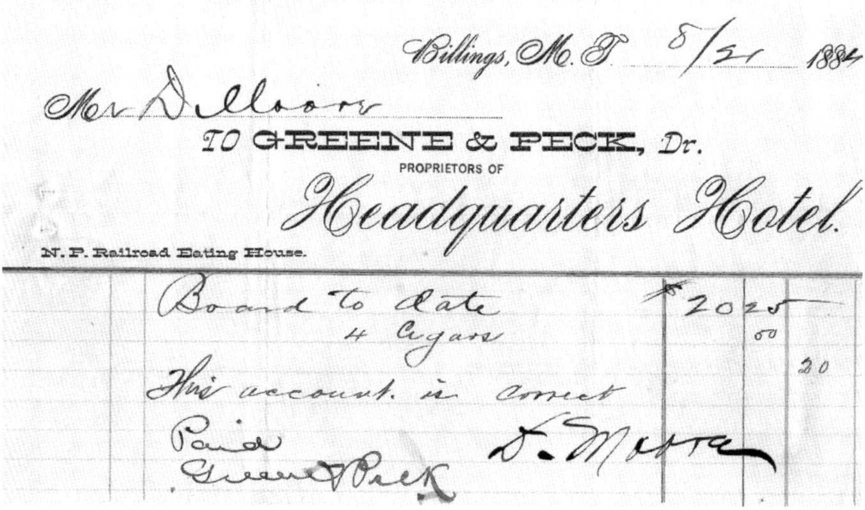
Billings, M. T. 8/21 1884
Mr D. Moore
TO GREENE & PECK, Dr.
PROPRIETORS OF
Headquarters Hotel
N. P. Railroad Eating House.
Board to date $20.25
4 Cigars 50
20
This account is correct
Paid
Greene & Peck
D. Moore

A receipt from the Headquarters Hotel for board and cigars, 1884. *Courtesy of James M. Reich.*

The attractive words "First-Class" lured customers to some of the initial dining establishments in Billings. The eateries included the Fulton Market Restaurant and the Vienna Bakery. One mile east of Billings in Coulson was Key City Dining Hall owned by Messrs. Potter and Aldrich. The eating venue was heralded as "A First-class Dining Hall, Where Meals will be served expeditiously, neatly and according to the taste of those who patronize them."

By the early summer of 1882, Potter and Aldrich, "who had been conducting the best restaurant at Coulson, became convinced of the fact that Billings proper was the place for their enterprise." They moved their eating establishment to be near the center of the emerging businesses and near the Headquarters Hotel, the first building in the town site constructed by the railroad, to accommodate the engineering staff of the "steel strands" through this area. The Dining Hall was the place to go for a "square meal," for "their bill of fare embraces everything that the market affords, and as one of the proprietors gives his personal attention to the conduct of the kitchen, guests may rest assured that orders are promptly and satisfactorily filled."

On September 10, 1882, proprietor of the Key City Dining Hall Edwin F. Potter left town under suspicious circumstances. Friends put up a reward of $3,000 for his return to Billings. "The sheriff pursued him, but at the present writing he has not been captured." A few weeks later, the restaurant reopened under the name of Key City European Restaurant with a new

European plan by T. Maylone, the former owner of the "Commercial restaurant, St. Louis, and recently of the St. James European restaurant at Bismarck. Wm. Morris and Paddy Donnelly are the artists of the culinary department." By the beginning of 1883, Messrs. R. Heney and Co. had purchased the business with Wardell and Co. as the new management team and boasted of "meals served all hours of the day or night."

The Fulton Market Restaurant, owned by H.J. Schmiel and Company, also offered "First-Class Meals" at all times of the day and night. The Vienna Bakery was a "New Line of Business for Billings" that was "Equal to the Establishments of the East," as it provided baked goods "unexcelled in quality and with the latest and most modern appointments." Vienna and rye bread were baked fresh every day and sold along with "First-class Bread, Pies, Cakes and Rolls."

By the fall of 1882, the *Billings Herald* reported there were three bakeries, four restaurants and one brewery with four lodging houses in town. The dining room at the Windsor Hotel opened in mid-August for the "best meal that Billings affords." Then, a month later, C.F. Yates purchased the dining room from H.S. Dodge with the belief "that under the new management the guests of the Windsor will have no reason to complain of the culinary arrangements." The restaurant, operated by the Forster brothers, advertised that it brought to Billings "long experience in catering to the public" with "sufficient guarantee that guests will be furnished with good meals." While the hotel was outfitted with "Spring Beds, Carpets and every other convenience peculiar to a first-class House," in the restaurant, the "table is supplied with all the delicacies of the season."

At the start, the Windsor Hotel served those who were arriving in Billings to work on the railway, on ranches and farms and in the mines. On Sunday night, November 19, 1882, the restaurant served a dinner that was "more than creditable, even in a frontier town noted for excellence of its restaurant. While endeavoring at all times to please their patrons, Messrs. Forster and Sons are bound to give the boys a good Sunday dinner if they do not make a cent." As time went on, the hotel became a gathering place for social events. On Independence Day 1884, "the ladies of the Congregational church will have a tent on the base ball ground where they will dispense ice cream, cake and lemonade and if strawberries can be procured they will likewise be served up." Later that afternoon, the women hosted an "ice cream festival" in the dining room.

By August, the Windsor was completing remodeling. "On the ground floor there will be a wide hall, and on its left will be the dining room, 59x19

Billings Brewing Company with a new electric sign and bottle-shaped car, 1910. *Courtesy of Billings Public Library.*

feet. On the north side will be a parlor 15x19, barber shop and bathrooms and kitchen. Up stairs will be 11 large bed-rooms, each provided with closet and heating apparatus."

Though eating venues were available, businesses selling wine, liquor and cigars were popular. The Florence, Burns Smith and Brown and Davis were some of the businesses offering libations and smokes for lifting the spirits of those in Billings. A year after the founding of the city, there were eleven saloons and three billiard halls on the main street. Prostitutes serviced gentlemen at "Social clubs" and "sporting houses," and the best-known lady of the night was Kit Rumley, who provided pleasure and incentive for the men to come into town. Early Sanborn maps of Billings labeled a solid lineup of "female boarding houses" along a two-and-a-half-block stretch of Minnesota Avenue.

The Rocky Mountain Brewery was in "full operation" with a German brewer who had learned the business in Baden, Germany, and had worked in breweries in both Austria and Milwaukee. The brewery touted that a good beer could be made on the Yellowstone River. At the end of August, the Western Brewery opened, proclaiming its beer as the best, and also offered "a fine lot of wine and liquors."

In 1900, the Billings Brewing Company opened at 2319 Montana Avenue in a three-story brick building. Created by Henry Mueller, Louis Best and Phil Grein, the brewing company stayed in business for over fifty years but was finally torn down in 1959. The facility processed twenty thousand barrels a year. In 1910, a forty- by twenty-five-foot electric sign beamed from the top of the building. The sign, lit by two thousand bulbs, showed the image of beer pouring from the brewery's Old Fashion Beer bottle. A beer bottle–shaped car reminiscent of an Oscar Mayer Wienermobile was seen around town and in parades. Horse-drawn cars loaded with Old Fashion Beers delivering the beverage to bars and saloons became familiar sightings on the streets of Billings. During Prohibition, in 1919, the brewery was forced to dump $11,876 worth of beer. At that time, the plant took on a new name, the Advance Manufacturing Co., and began producing a bottled cereal drink called Top Notch. Unfortunately, the brewery that once made Milwaukee jealous of its beer with its brand "Old Fashion Beer" never picked up momentum after 1933. Attempts at advertisement promoted Old Fashion Beer "as a food for the tired, weak, overwrought nerves…brings roses to the cheeks…builds blood and tissues, soothes, quiets and strengthens the nerves, and is highly recommended in many cases by eminent physicians." By the end of World War II, with old and faulty equipment, the company produced contaminated and poorly carbonated beer, which eventually led to its downfall.

The saloons provided the haven for the single men who were arriving. Whether they were seeking adventure or fortune or both, many had left more civilized and comfortable lives behind in the East. The saloons provided a temporary place to stay, but they mostly provided a sense of community where the men could gather to seek camaraderie and support. If not a place to lift their spirits, they were a place to take refuge and nourish their hunger.

The Headquarters Restaurant, located on North Twenty-fifth Street, provided a place for "Rest for the Weary" after it secured a large supply of cots in the early summer of 1882. It was "prepared to furnish excellent Beds for those who want to enjoy a good night's rest," as there were "No Hard Bunks in the Future." The establishment was the first building in the Billings town site and the first hostelry when it was built in May 1882 to house the engineering staff working with the Northern Pacific Railway. The hotel was moved to the north side of the tracks to the end of North Twenty-eighth Street and opened to the general public until it burned down in 1891.

In 1883, water was available in a "constant supply into the hotel whenever it may be required." The Headquarters was the landmark that other businesses used to reference their location, and it served as the engineers' administrative center for the Northern Pacific Railway during the construction work. It was said that "All Trains Stop at this Hotel (and the Railway Eating House) for Meals." In the spring of 1883, the Headquarters dining room underwent remodeling with re-plastering and "was greatly enlarged by the removal of the partition between it and the adjoining rooms."

The dining room provided for social events in all definitions of the word. On one occasion, "the young ladies of the dining room at the Headquarters hotel" gave a party and "enjoyed themselves 'tripping the light fantastic' until an early hour." "The negro banjoist, violinist and cornetist, W.H. McKanlass, showed in the dining room." On a Sunday evening in the early summer of 1883, "Chief Moses accompanied by a number of Spokane Indians passed east on the train bound for Washington." It was reported that "the red men dined at the Headquarters and conducted themselves at the table as if they were accustomed to the use of knives, forks and napkins, and all the other appliances of a modern dining table." F.L. Greene and W.L. Peck were determined to ensure that "guests will find that the Accommodations are FIRST-CLASS in every particular." In 1884, the hotel opened a new dining area that was composed of "exceeding cheerful looking rooms" with elegantly displayed heads of buffalo, elk and mountain sheep. Across the hall from the dining was a ladies' parlor.

In the years after the founding of Billings, establishments came and went. Foster and Son's Restaurant had "Always on hand, Oysters, Chickens and Game," while the Office Restaurant and Saloon offered "Choice Steaks, Spring Chicken, Saddle Rock Oysters, Game of all Kinds, Lunch of all Kinds" and, of course, "The Best Wines and Liquors in Montana." The Magnolia Hotel, owned by A.E. Hertzell, advertised having the "Best Meals in Town," while the hotel was the "Headquarters for Traveling and Commercial Men." On the south side of the track, opposite the depot, was Mrs. Preble's Restaurant, where a refreshing dish of ice cream was served.

By 1882, "the track of the Northern Pacific railroad [had] reached the bank of the Yellowstone River opposite of town." The job of raising one large hammer to hit a spike required strength and accuracy. "At noon all the crews return to the dining cars, where they are most bountifully fed

A postcard of the Northern Pacific lunchroom in the foreground with the waiting room, baggage handling and ticketing in the building in the background. *Courtesy of Billings Public Library.*

and allowed to rest during the full noon time." The dining car was the last in the line of the trains. "The dining and kitchen cars are all 'double deckers,' that is two stories in height, the upper story of each being used as sleeping apartments."

Dining cars were available for tourist travel in the early summer of 1883. "The bills of fare will be first class in every particular, far superior to the accommodations usually afforded the ordinary eating stations on the lines of the railroads." The meals cost seventy-five cents and were served at "regular hours" even if the train was not running on time. General passenger agent Barnes reported great patronage, with the largest money take at $160. The poor behavior of the staff led the Northern Pacific to issue "orders forbidding the sale of liquors on dining to anyone except passengers. The officers and employees of the trains are therefore put off from getting an inspiring glass except by making a hurried trip to the nearest saloon when they stop at stations." One can only imagine the juxtapositioning of officers and workers at the exits of the train as they approached a station.

In 1909, the Billings Depot was built, a $65,000 passenger station to service three railroad companies: Northern Pacific; Great Northern; and Chicago, Burlington and Quincy. The building was designed in the Beaux

The Northern Pacific lunchroom provided a comfortable place to refuel, relax and read from 1909 to 1965. *Courtesy of James M. Reich.*

Arts Eclectic style and housed a lunchroom, mail building and office building, with only the Livingston Depot equaling this station in style. Passengers could relax here while waiting for trains to carry them to their destinations, and locals could stop here for a break in the day for respite or a bite to eat. The "lunch house," in its own separate building, employed a chef to run the kitchen. The lunchroom finally closed in 1965.

In 1902, the Billings Investment Company provided funding for the building of the Northern Hotel at the corner of North Broadway and First Avenue North; it would manage the property until 1971. When doors opened in 1904, the Northern Hotel began decades of celebrations and time-marked events. The hotel burned in 1940, to be reopened in 1942. The famed Golden Belle Restaurant opened in 1959 and served food and spirits until it closed permanently in 2006. The Northern Hotel, rebirthed by Mike and Chris Nelson in 2013, returned, anchored by two restaurants: TEN and Bernie's Diner.

Finally, the McCormick Hotel at 2419 and the Carlin Hotel at 2501 require mention, as the buildings still exist on modern-day Montana Avenue. Moreover, the past proprietors had profound impacts on the prosperity and progress of Billings. The McCormick, built in 1905, reopened as the McCormick Café in 1998, while the Carlin Hotel, built in September 1913, served as a canteen during World War I and then as a nightclub, Club Carlin;

a restaurant, Q Cuisine; and an extended-stay hotel, Carlin Hotel, in the early 1990s. William H. McCormick, born in Wisconsin, was the nephew of Paul McCormick, who was known as "the grand old man of Montana" for being one of the notable builders of business in Billings. In 1907, the younger McCormick established the McCormick of Montana Seed House, which became one of the largest seed houses in the state. The company handled hay, grain and seeds, as well as poultry supplies, and specialized in the grading of beans. It had more than one hundred employees. Parley G. Carlin was a prominent real estate owner, while his brother William Hobart Carlin, a café owner and cook, made news when he drove his Jewett two thousand miles to Lorain, Ohio, and back in "high gear" the entire way. Unfortunately, both McCormick and Carlin died tragic deaths. P.G. Carlin committed suicide by shooting himself, presumably defeated by his fight to heal after a "paralytic stroke," and W.H. McCormick, "for reasons unknown, hung himself on September 12, 1936."

The Golden Belle Dining Room in the Northern Hotel, "one of the outstanding restaurants in the Northwest," 1960s. *Courtesy of James M. Reich.*

Both of these men lived in a period when Billings was booming as a town. Unfortunately, they could not embrace all the possibilities. In the 1918 Jackson Real Estate Directory, President and Manager John C. Roberts of Roberts Realty, Inc., extolled Billings as the next great city of the Northwest located in the "Great Midland Empire of Montana." The empire included 900,000 acres of irrigated land with 5 million acres of "rich" unirrigated land. Overnight fortunes were to be made here, as there existed "more acres

The McCormick Hotel was originally built in 1905 by William H. McCormick. *Courtesy of Billings Public Library.*

of coal lands than the state of Pennsylvania," and the great oil fields that opened fifty miles south of Billings were "real gushers." The town with seven large business blocks was readily accessible, with twenty-eight daily passenger trains moving in and out of the township of twenty thousand people.

Billings may have been nicknamed the Magic City, which allowed for limitless opportunities, but magic also implied that the possibilities were not always apparent. Living and surviving in what has now been rebranded as "Montana's Trailhead" required creativity, versatility and tenacity. It was no wonder that the likes of Buffalo Bill Cody helped H. Alfred Heimer start the Rex or that Calamity Jane, before packing "up her Saratoga and [leaving] our city," owned a restaurant on the south side. Those who made a mark on the city by the Yellowstone River did so with much hard work. But Billings always possessed a groundedness tempered with some modesty, which was reflected in its approach to food, though these days, the world's flavors are slowly infusing into Big Sky flavors.

2

THE TRUE FAIRY TALE OF THE NORTHERN HOTEL AND THE GOLDEN BELLE

Once upon a time, in 1904, in the then Magic City, two princes—Henry W. Rowley and P.B. Moss—built the Northern Hotel at First Avenue North and Broadway. With monies and treasures from the Billings Investment Company, a sixty-nine-room hotel was erected. Soon, travelers, prospectors and dreamers came from near and far to the Italian Renaissance–style three-story building. With an architecture of symmetry, geometry and order, "the most modern hotel in Montana" welcomed guests through a portico flanked by Greek Ionic columns. A double loggia on the second and third floors formed a protected platform for viewing life on the street and the comings and goings of distinguished guests.

The Northern Hotel mesmerized all people, common and royal, for soon it became the social center for the city. Those who arrived at the hotel for dinner on March 7, 1909, experienced food fit for kings and queens. The "Sunday Dinner Menu" began with "Caviar Canape. Blue Point Cocktail. Celery. Radishes. Olives," followed by "Consomme in Cup. Oxtail with Sherry." Next came a selection of fish, chicken and meat dishes with accompaniments: "Fillet of Sole—Tartar Sauce—Sliced Cucumbers—Saratoga Chips…Fried Spring Chicken, Maryland—Cauliflower…Roast Prime Ribs of Beef or Spring Lamb—Currant Jelly—Mashed Potatoes—Browned Sweet Potatoes—Garden Peas." As in the custom of European dining, the next course was a salad, and this night the offering was "Tomato and Lettuce Salad." "Apple Tapioca Pudding. Coconut Pie. Caramel Ice Cream. Assorted Cake. Neufchatel

Above: A postcard of the Northern Hotel, "the Largest and Finest Hotel in Montana," 1960s. *Courtesy of Billings Public Library.*

Left: The cover of the children's menu from the Northern Hotel. *Courtesy of the Northern Hotel.*

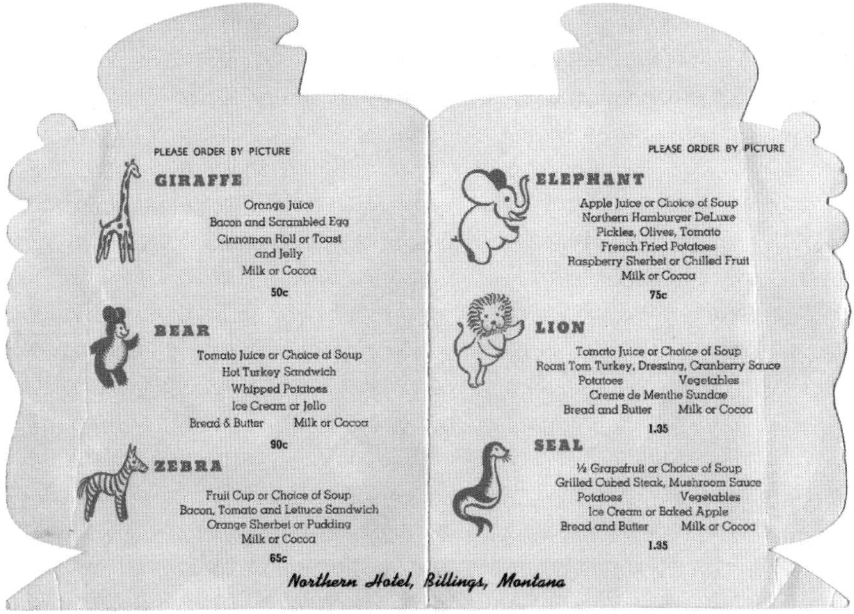

The inside of the children's menu from the Northern Hotel. *Courtesy of the Northern Hotel.*

Cheese and Crackers" made up the dessert selections, accompanied with a choice of coffee.

About a year later, to encourage male downtown workers to come in to eat, an ad announced, "Beginning Monday, January 3, the Northern Hotel will serve its business men's lunch from 12 to 2 every day except Sundays, for which they will pay 35 cents." To attract the ladies to the hotel, the Northern added another wing with a tearoom in 1912. Two years later, a new marble-lined lobby and atrium was added to provide an elegant place for entering and gathering. Finally, a fourth floor, with a Mansard roof shading pedimented dormers, was added in 1916, high above the Billings land.

In the next years, many banquets and elaborate celebrations took place at the Northern. Theodore Roosevelt stayed at the hotel in 1918 and President Woodrow Wilson in 1919. In June 1924, the Kyote class of Billings High School held its annual banquet in the tearoom, honoring the winning of the state championship in journalism. "The banquet table was beautifully decorated with tulips, lilacs, flags and honeysuckle and each member found at his place card a neat little folder of brown and gold color design containing the menu, toasts, and appropriate illuminations depicting cowboys and accessories, the motif of the annual." Song and dance resounded in the tearoom with music programs when Mrs. O.L. Koppe and Mrs. E.O. Price hosted fifty guests. In the room beautifully decorated with peonies, Mr. Franklyn Hunt entertained with songs, joined by others for a two-hour program. For celebrating a "birthday anniversary," "Mrs. Lynn Holliday entertained on Saturday last with a delightful 1 o'clock luncheon…Yellow and orchid color tones were carried out in the decorations and after partaking of a delicious menu the afternoon was spent with bridge."

By 1940, the Northern Hotel had spent more than $600,000 expanding and renovating. With two hundred rooms for ladies and gentlemen, the hotel was "rated as one of the finest hostelries in the West." Inside the Northern, other businesses included "Buy for Less Drug Store, a jewelry store, beauty and barber shop, the Jane Drake Dress Shop, a millinery, Helmer's Oak Tavern, the Northern Grill, a billiard parlor, and offices of the Northern Pacific and Burlington railways, the Dude Ranchers' Association and Northwest Airlines."

At about 4:40 p.m. on September 11, 1940, smoke and flames shot from the basement of the dress store. Bad luck huffed and puffed the building completely down. "No clues to the cause of the disastrous blaze had been established, but Fire Chief V.H. Steele said he was investigating several 'stories and rumors,' that he had heard." One story was that an explosion had occurred before the fire. To this day, no cause has been established.

Within weeks, the Billings Investment Company, with P.B. Moss as president, had hired the Chicago architectural firm Holabird and Root to design a ten-story hotel. On July 7, 1942, Manager Lester Carter opened the doors of the hotel to reveal terrazzo floors inlaid with brass on the basement and first floors, pastel-colored walls, exposed columns and travertine marble walls in the entry vestibules.

The hotel housed the lobby and shops on the first floor along with a dining room, kitchen, coffee shop and cocktail lounge called the Frontier Bar. The lounge was an interpretation of an old railway depot scene with red walls featuring a western-themed mural by Catherine O'Brien. "The lobby is treated on one wall with tufted leather in off-white color, and the other surfaces are in walnut flexwood. The seating is arranged so as to provide a congenial meeting place for guests, much like the lounge of a club." It featured brown, red and off-white leather-covered chairs and sofas with end tables with "highly-decorated lamps of red design."

The main dining room on the first floor was carpeted in green of a modern leaf design, with walls the color of "straw." Natural birch-finished and yellow-colored armchairs seated fifty-two people comfortably. Venetian blinds covered the windows, and Civil War prints adorned the walls. The coffee shop, adjoining the dining room, with an asphalt tile floor and slate gray walls, could seat seventy at the tables and twenty more at the counter.

Donald J. McCrea, a graduate of Carlton College in Northfield, Minnesota, and the University of Minnesota hotel course, had been employed at the Florence Hotel in Missoula. At the Northern, he had the opportunity to oversee events in the ballroom that now accommodated three hundred guests. Measuring sixty-one by thirty-four feet, it was the largest individual room in the hotel. A panel of windows facing the southwest was covered with heavy drapes that disappeared into special pockets. A private dining room equipped with a kitchen accessed the main kitchen on the first floor via service stairs and an elevator.

The hotel was ventilated with a fresh air supply fan and an exhaust fan. The system drew air from outside and then discharged it. A refrigerating air conditioning system cooled the air. The conditioning system also held heating coils so the spaces could be supplied with heat and cold for ultimate comfort. The heating system included two boilers that provided heating throughout, including responding to individual thermostat settings from each room.

The open house attracted three thousand guests to tour the new building. Carter invited the "greatest assemblage of high-class talent to be brought together in Billings in some time." Eclectic acts such as Kenny Jagger,

A gravy bowl and teacup and saucer from the Northern Hotel. *Courtesy of James M. Reich.*

The cover of the Northern Hotel menu with photograph taken by Chas J. Beldon, a Wyoming photographer and rancher. *Courtesy of James M. Reich.*

who played the Hammond organ and piano simultaneously; the Three Ambassadors musical trio; the Serranos, a South American dance company; and Beverly Morrell and Company, a novelty Hollywood roller-skating troupe, entertained all those who ventured to the Northern Hotel.

During the war years, the Northern Hotel housed one hundred soldiers in Billings on special training and opened a "service man club"

Inside the Golden Belle Saloon with red burgundy décor and a nude painting on the back wall, circa 1960. *Courtesy of the Western Heritage Center.*

that promoted dances and other entertainment. The third and fourth floors of the hotel were not finished until 1945 because of World War II. When the Northern Hotel was complete, it consisted of an estimated 245 guest rooms. The facility housed a restaurant, coffee shop and cocktail lounge, along with other shops and businesses.

For Mother's Day dinner on May 13, 1956, at a cost of $2.50, a buffet was served from noon until 9:00 p.m. Mom and family could select exotic items such as "Chilled Mandarin Orange Cocktail, Marinated Herring Cocktail and Cream of Chicken Soup a la Reina." In the entree category, "Maitre d'Hotel Roast Long Island Duckling with Wild Rice Dressing, Brandy Sauce" with sides of "Ginger bread" bordered on the unusual, while sweet endings included French Strawberry Cream Pie and Hawaiian Pineapple Sundae.

On September 12, 1959, the Northern Hotel opened the famed Golden Belle restaurant. Carter and his secretary and innkeeper, Joseph Callihan, spent between $70,000 and $80,000 remodeling the restaurant and cocktail lounge. They eliminated the Old West theme and brought in burgundy-colored walls and carpeting accented with fixtures and decorations from the 1890s. Décor included paintings by Ken Ralston of Billings from the late nineteenth century. There was a vintage nickelodeon

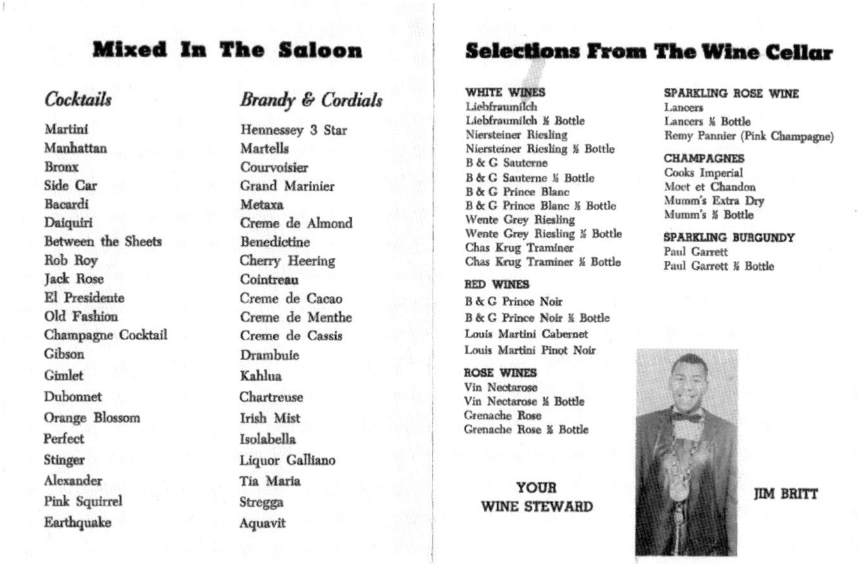

Mixed In The Saloon

Cocktails

Martini
Manhattan
Bronx
Side Car
Bacardi
Daiquiri
Between the Sheets
Rob Roy
Jack Rose
El Presidente
Old Fashion
Champagne Cocktail
Gibson
Gimlet
Dubonnet
Orange Blossom
Perfect
Stinger
Alexander
Pink Squirrel
Earthquake

Brandy & Cordials

Hennessey 3 Star
Martells
Courvoisier
Grand Marinier
Metaxa
Creme de Almond
Benedictine
Cherry Heering
Cointreau
Creme de Cacao
Creme de Menthe
Creme de Cassis
Drambuie
Kahlua
Chartreuse
Irish Mist
Isolabella
Liquor Galliano
Tia Maria
Stregga
Aquavit

Selections From The Wine Cellar

WHITE WINES
Liebfraumilch
Liebfraumilch ½ Bottle
Niersteiner Riesling
Niersteiner Riesling ½ Bottle
B & G Sauterne
B & G Sauterne ½ Bottle
B & G Prince Blanc
B & G Prince Blanc ½ Bottle
Wente Grey Riesling
Wente Grey Riesling ½ Bottle
Chas Krug Traminer
Chas Krug Traminer ½ Bottle

RED WINES
B & G Prince Noir
B & G Prince Noir ½ Bottle
Louis Martini Cabernet
Louis Martini Pinot Noir

ROSE WINES
Vin Nectarose
Vin Nectarose ½ Bottle
Grenache Rose
Grenache Rose ½ Bottle

SPARKLING ROSE WINE
Lancers
Lancers ½ Bottle
Remy Pannier (Pink Champagne)

CHAMPAGNES
Cooks Imperial
Moet et Chandon
Mumm's Extra Dry
Mumm's ½ Bottle

SPARKLING BURGUNDY
Paul Garrett
Paul Garrett ½ Bottle

YOUR
WINE STEWARD

JIM BRITT

Mixed drinks and wine selections from the Golden Belle with wine steward Jim Britt, 1950s. *Courtesy of the Northern Hotel.*

The drinks and wine menu from the Golden Belle, 1950s. *Courtesy of the Northern Hotel.*

player piano. Designer Ross Cox, with Western Hotels, Inc., was credited with the interior design. Bartenders sported long-handled moustaches and vests, while the waitresses dressed like Mae West from the set of *My Little Chickadee*. Carter and Callihan enlisted Chef Al Bohley's talents in the kitchen and James Britt's finesse as the wine steward.

On opening day, a writer for "Business News" in the *Billings Gazette* commented that the "eye-catching art, aside from the feminine clientele, is a large painting known as Golden Belle whence the establishment takes its name." The writer continued on to describe that "the chandeliers especially designed for the Belle, are similar to those which lighted the capers of newly minted millionaires in San Francisco 15 years before the earthquake of 1906."

Carter and Callihan promoted the Golden Belle as a high-end alternative to many of the other eateries in downtown Billings. A full-page ad was taken out in the *Billings Gazette* on the day of the opening. The gist of the promotion was a "monument to the capitalistic system" and invited Soviet premier Nikita Khrushchev:

> *The uncollected people of Montana send to the collectivized peasants of the Union of the Soviet Socialist Republics and suggest that there is no more logical place to hold a frank exchange of views and heart-to-heart talks in a summit meeting than the Golden Belle restaurant and bar which is now open for meetings, trysts, and other convivialities.*

Many reasons were cited for why the Golden Belle was the logical place for Khrushchev to come, but the main reason was the "capitalistic" food and meals. Specialties included shish kebabs, South African lobster and baby beef T-bone steak. Priced at $3.75, complete dinners included a soup tureen, salad bowl, beverage and dessert. For about the same price, a diner could choose "Disjointed Country Fried Chicken with Chicken Gravy and Whipped Potato; Broiled Ground Sirloin Steak with French Fried Onion Rings, vegetable and potato; Fresh Rocky Mountain Trout, Hash Brown Potato and garden vegetable." Khrushchev never did come, but the tongue-in-cheek humor continued.

For the days before the opening and weeks after, the Golden Belle ran captivating ads with intriguing questions with answers from Joseph Burnie Callihan. Inquiries such as "What are they up to in Butte?" to "Are they making trouble for us up in Helena?" to "Why is limestone lettuce plucked only by tender maidens and hastened to the Golden Belle in aerocraft restricted to low altitudes?" were posed. Adjacent to

Bartender *Benny Stoelting* and cocktail waitress *June Nelson* seem to be enjoying themselves. The Gay Nineties costumes blend in with the Golden Belle decor.

Wine steward *James Britt* pours for a pleased guest.

Two of the major reasons for the distinguished food served in the Golden Belle Restaurant: Chef *Al Bohley* and pantry chef *Mike Di Lulo*.

Assistant manager *Ed Parks* of the Golden Belle chats with guests.

Attractive desk clerks *Erna Parker*, left, and *Betty Kinnick*, along with bellman *Glen Starkweather* give their VSP Service smiles a workout.

10

From *FRONT!*, a magazine for western hotels, January–February 1960. *Courtesy of the Northern Hotel.*

the question was always a sketch that required contemplation. The answers were written as though you were sitting down and talking to the innkeeper. In answer to the question, "Is it absolutely required that Shish Kebab be served the HONOR GUEST when one gathers for a celebration at the Golden Belle?" the entire ritual was described: "While you and your friends sit there smiling like visiting royalty, the Shish Kebab entourage, led by J. Arthur White, sweeps into view. The gong sounds, the Northern lights grow dim, and the ritual has begun."

Carter, a native New Yorker, moved to Billings on a cold January day in 1955 with his wife, Hannelore. From his father, Greek immigrant Herecles Kinokidos, he learned the restaurant business, with further training at New York University's Hotel Management School. For thirty-four years, Carter, who became known as "Mr. Northern Hotel," worked at the Northern Hotel, "greeting travelers at the registration desk, schmoozing in the Golden Belle Saloon, stopping by to chat up guests in the restaurant...He always looked immaculate in his New York suits and silk ties. His old-world charm was legendary."

It was during Carter's time that Richard M. Nixon stayed at the hotel. While campaigning for the presidency, Nixon arrived in Billings shortly before midnight on October 8, 1960. After greeting about three thousand people, the vice president retired to a room on the tenth floor and, "although he did not go to bed until well after midnight, was up about 7 a.m., dressed quickly and told the secret service agents assigned to his protection that he wanted to go out alone." Nixon walked to the Squire Restaurant and ordered a breakfast of "hotcakes, a local sausage, milk and coffee."

According to Mike Nelson, who purchased the Northern Hotel in 2009 with his brother, Carter was a man "who really believed in the old style of hospitality." When someone of importance arrived at the hotel, it was the general manager's responsibility to be on hand to personally cater to the guest. With Nixon's coming to the hotel, Carter called his wife and requested her to bring him new clothes, as he knew he would be staying at the Northern for an undetermined amount of time. Hannelore made a strudel and brought it with some clothes. She got past the bodyguards and managed to get Nixon the pastry. He lost the election for presidency, but in January, he sent Hannelore a note thanking her for the treat, signing the note, "Yours Truly, Dick."

In 1973, when F. Jack Anderson reigned as vice-president and general manager, the Golden Belle won the "Holiday Award" for Distinctive Food and Beverages. Everything from "Crab Legs Mediterranean" to "Roast Duckling en Brochete" enticed couples to savor dinners for two "when you're celebrating something special. Or just out for the evening." The photo in an ad found in the *Polk City Directory* showed a wine steward with a neatly folded white napkin draped over his forearm as he showed a bottle of chianti in a woven basket to a couple. The man looked adoringly at his date while she was captivated by the wine service. The Golden

Waitresses at the Golden Belle in the Northern Hotel. Third from the right is Doris Waddell, late 1950s. *Courtesy of Karen Waddell.*

Belle continued to be a popular gathering and eating place until it closed permanently in 2006.

Karen Waddell and her mother, Doris, both worked at the Golden Belle. Karen waitressed in the lounge in the early 1970s, while her mother began waiting tables in the Golden Belle beginning shortly after it opened in 1959. Karen recalled working with Red Burnett, the bartender and manager of the bar. "Everyone said he was going to die behind the bar" because he was so dedicated to his job. She described him as "gruff but he was great. He was funny." She shared how Burnett would have the staff constantly "roaring with laughter" with his stories when they sat down together after the lunch rush. Karen shared a story of how he accommodated guests by

A waitress at the Northern Hotel in the Golden Belle, 1970s. *Courtesy of Northern Hotel.*

bringing a bottle of bubby to their room and ended up in the bathtub with them with his clothes on. Addison Bragg, who chronicled life in Billings for over half a century, told of "our town's most prestigious watering hole," where Burnett had a habit of matching silver dollars with bar patrons during the lunch hour. The fun continued with customers as the staff got dressed up for holidays, with Karen recalling how she donned a bunny suit for an Easter celebration.

Starting a year after the Golden Belle opened, the Billings Petroleum Club assembled in the newly completed annex, where it operated for

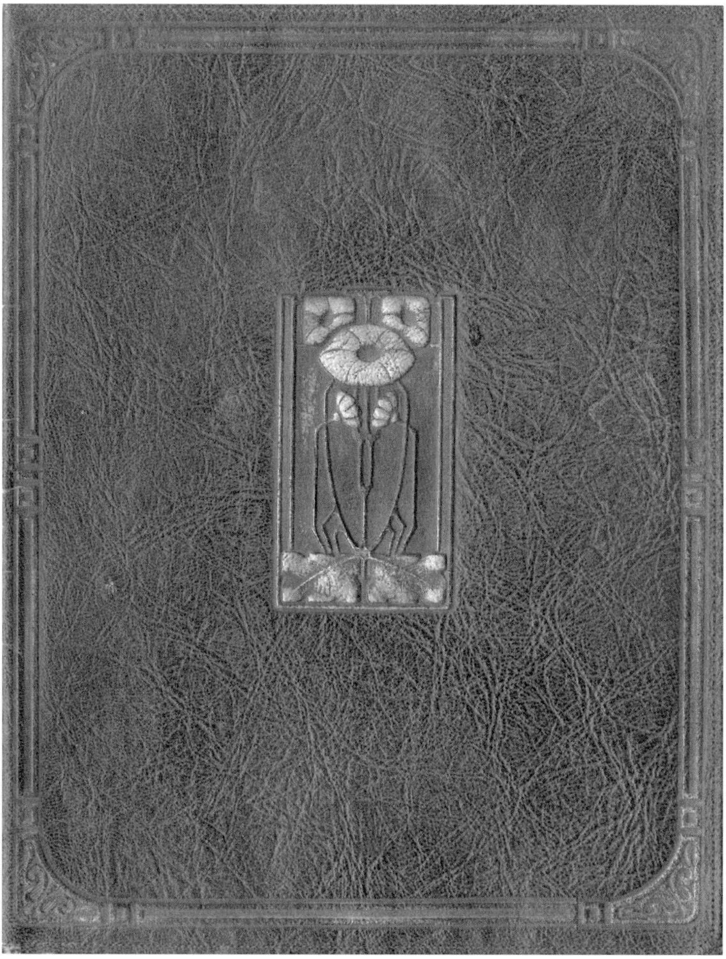

The embossed leather menu cover from the Northern Hotel, circa 1920s. *Courtesy of the Northern Hotel.*

twenty years. The club, incorporated in 1954 during the oil boom years in Montana and Wyoming, originally limited membership to the oil industry. In 1959, the basement became the space for a lunch and dinner club used for meetings and social gatherings, with the larger Carter Room on the first floor able to cater larger events.

On January 9, 2009, Chris and Mike Nelson purchased the Northern Hotel for $2,475,090, outbidding the amount of the creditor's representative, Missoula CPA Dennis Minemyer, by $1 at a foreclosure sale. On March 15, 2013, the new Northern opened its state-of-the-art

A card from Don and Kim Olsen, Mike Mathew and Kay Foster to Mike and Chris Nelson for the 2013 opening of the Northern Hotel. *Courtesy of the Northern Hotel.*

hotel with two restaurants: Bernie's Diner and TEN. Bernie's Diner, named after Mike and Chris's mother, serves breakfast and lunch, including the Northern's Monte Cristo sandwich. TEN focuses on fine dining and takes its name from the owners' father, Thomas Edgar Nelson. The restaurant originally opened with the talents of Executive Chef Eric Stenberg, but these days, Executive Chef Tim Freeman works on giving Billings and Montana a "global presence in the culinary world." He creates dishes using local ingredients, including wild game.

Chris and Mike Nelson had come full circle, returning to the kingdom where they spent their childhood. They were destined to rule the Northern Hotel; it seems they have always had a connection. Their grandfather Harvey Schutrop installed the hotel's switchboard before it burned in 1940. Their late parents were longtime Billings business owners. Chris graduated from Senior High School, while Mike attended West High. Mike celebrated with his family at the Golden Belle after he asked his wife for her hand in marriage. Mike is currently the general manager of the Northern, while Chris continues to run Zoot Enterprises, a bank credit check operation in Bozeman.

Mike Nelson had a goal in mind when bringing the Northern Hotel into a new life: "We wanted the people of Billings to gather here. We wanted it to take the place as the meeting place of Billings again. We wanted it to be important to the people of Billings. We want the Northern to be a Billings hotel first, Montana second and then the rest of the U.S."

The Northern Hotel is once again the castle for all to enter. With the powers of the two modern princes, Mike and Chris Nelson, the hotel is the magical place that will continue to make those who enter live happily forever after.

3
DINING AND DANCING

Elmo Club, Skyline Club, Windmill, Stock Exchange and Others

She smacked her lips together for the final check in the mirror before leaving for a night of dining and dancing. As she smoothed the flare of her dress, her date gently placed a fur stole over her shoulders. The air of his Old Spice melded with her Chanel as they headed out to a supper club to meet friends. Once a week on Friday night, they sipped cocktails before dining on simple American fare or fancy gourmet food and then danced the night away.

Back in the 1930s and into the late 1970s, one got all dolled up to go out for a night of dining and dancing. Addison Bragg wrote about after-dark dining in the Magic City in "Dining of Yesteryear Recalled" in the *Billings Gazette*: Those who spent "the shank of most of their nights on the town preferred Bob Porter's Turf, Gert Egan's Vegas Club, the Beacon, Louis and 'Mug's,' Eastman's Windmill, the Elmo Club, and the Skyline Club on the Rims west of the Airport." When Billings' citizens such as Chuck Hauptman and Pete Zagorda were asked of dining and dancing memories from the past, the Skyline and Elmo Clubs were best remembered, along with the Windmill Club. Then, in the late '70s, the Stock Exchange became a popular disco hangout.

An aerial view of the Elmo Club on Lake Elmo, 1940s. *Courtesy of James M. Reich.*

The Elmo Club

In the Magic City, the "shank" activities became synonymous with the name Robert James "Bob" Porter. From oil fields to truck driving and road construction, Porter converted to work in restaurants, bars, nightclubs and gambling houses. With that experience, he took over the Elmo Club in 1945. After Porter passed away on May 7, 1993, his obituary stated, "Few in the restaurant business were able to match Bob Porter when it came to sensing and answering needs and demands of the public, especially that part of it out for the traditional 'night on the town.' When it came to food, drink, entertainment and service, Porter had few peers."

Lake Elmo, located five miles north of Billings, was originally built as a storage basin for irrigation water in 1906 and continues in that capacity to this day. The sixty-four-acre reservoir was originally called Holling Lake. Elmo and Miriam McCracken were the owners of the lake at the time it opened for recreational use in 1929. They built a two-story nightclub on the

The shore view of the Elmo Club on Lake Elmo, 1940s. *Courtesy of Billings Public Library.*

lake's north side that became a social center and musicians' hub. Chicken and steak dinners made it a popular eating venue.

The Elmo Club opened on May 12, 1930, becoming one of the hot spots of the '30s and '40s. When the dance pavilion held its grand opening a year later, blues singer Jackie Sherman and Tommy Ferguson and his Tavern Orchestra entertained the crowds. Aside from eats and beats, the Elmo Club "was noted for its gambling tables where '21' was dealt by Bob Oliver and Ira Johnson, and its bar behind which Chuck Campbell was a regular." On August 31, 1945, the McCrackens sold the club to Alpha J. Olsen and Agnes I. Porter, the wives of Howard Olsen and Bob Porter. After the building burned in 1946, Porter moved the club to Laurel Road, as he lacked the funds to rebuild on Lake Elmo. Agnes and Bob ended their marriage in 1948.

Porter's ego reached the skies. His famous sign in front of the new Elmo Club was a landmark for years. As it was, the forty-eight-foot, two-inch-high sign, including the concrete base, was the tallest sign in Montana at the time, a result of Porter's request that the neon company find the tallest sign in the state

Left: The cover of the Elmo Club menu, with Bob Porter standing under his giant neon sign from the late 1940s. *Courtesy of James M. Reich.*

Below: The diverse and eclectic Elmo Club menu from the late 1940s. *Courtesy of James M. Reich.*

We Specialize in . . .
BANQUETS AND PRIVATE PARTIES
. . . and will do everything in our power to show your guests an enjoyable evening!

Italian Dinners

Meat Balls & Spaghetti $2.00
Mushrooms & Spaghetti $2.00
Raviolas & Spaghetti $2.00
Italian Chicken with Raviolas & Spaghetti $2.50

Chinese Dishes

We are particularly proud of our Chinese Cuisine . . . the reason will be obvious once you have tried it.

Sweet and Sour Ribs with Steamed Rice $2.50
Shrimp, Chinese Style $3.00
Steak Rice, a la Louie $2.50
Pork Fried Rice with Mushrooms $2.75

All Entrees on This Menu May Be Ordered
A LA CARTE
at 50c Less Than Complete Dinner
This Includes
POTATOES ROLLS
BEVERAGE

TRY ONE OF OUR INDIVIDUAL WINES TO START YOUR DINNER RIGHT

Elmo Supper Club Entrees

OUR MEAT Is All Choice Deluxe, Cut and Prepared Right Here at the Club by Our Own Experts. Feel Free to Inspect Our Kitchen and Butcher Shop at Any Time.

All Steaks and Chops Will Be Charcoal Broiled Upon Request
Choice of Oil and Vinegar, Elmo Club Dressing, French Dressing or Roquefort Dressing

COMPLETE DINNERS

CHATEAUBRIAND Prepared for Two—with Sauce Bereau $9.00
Choice Tenderloin Strip, Broiled and Planked, European Style
PORTER'S SPECIAL TWIN STEAK Spiked with Bob's Special Sauce $7.00
LAMB RACK COMPLETE DINNER FOR TWO $7.00
Broiled and Planked, with Mint Sauce — All Steaks on Sizzlers
FULL CUT SIRLOIN STEAK FOR TWO $6.75

Kuda Steak Marinated in Wine $5.00
Corn Fed T-Bone 32 Oz. Natural Sauce $5.50
Filet Mignon Smothered in Mushrooms $4.50
Marinated Steak With Wine Sauce $4.00
Full Cut Tenderloin Bereau Sauce $4.00
New York Cut Sirloin Natural Bone in 16 oz. $3.75
Choice Top Sirloin $3.50
Spring Lamb Chops Mint Jelly $3.00
Roast Prime Ribs Au Jus $3.00
Elmo Club Steak Mushroom Sauce $2.75
Chopped Tenderloin Steak Mushroom Sauce $2.50

GRILLED LITTLE PIG CHOPS WITH SPICED APPLE $2.50
HAM STEAK, PINEAPPLE GLACE, HONEY BUTTER $2.50
BREADED PORK TENDERLOIN, SPICED PEAR $2.00
BARBECUED RIBS $2.50

All Our Chicken Is PAN FRIED IN BUTTER . . . Our Chickens FRESH DAILY . . . Absolutely NOT Frozen.
PAN FRIED CHICKEN $2.75
HOT BISCUITS AND HONEY

French Fried Onions Per Order .... .75
Our Special Stuffed BAKED POTATO has taken us a long time and a lot of effort to perfect . . . we hope it pleases you.
Mushroom Sauce .... .50
Sauce Bereau .... .75
Spanish .... .50

ROCK CORNISH GAME HEN $3.50
CHICKEN A LA KIEV Succulent Breast of Chicken Garnished With Half of Peach and Sour Cream $3.00
CHICKEN IN BASKET $1.75
TENDERLOIN STEAK SANDWICH $2.00

SEAFOODS

LOBSTER THERMIDOR OR NEWBERG $3.25
LOUISIANA FROG LEGS, with Tartar Sauce and Drawn Butter $3.25
BROILED AFRICAN LOBSTER TAILS, Drawn Butter $3.50
OCEAN SPRAY SHRIMP, Shredded Lettuce, Tartar or Cocktail Sauce $2.50
FRESH WEST COAST CRACKED CRAB, Mayonnaise $2.50
PORTER'S FAMOUS CRAB LOUIE $2.50
FRESH RAINBOW TROUT, Rasher or Bacon $2.50
DEEP SEA SCALLOPS, Cole Slaw and Tartar Sauce $2.00

TAX NOT INCLUDED

A la Carte

Large Assorted Relish Tray $4.00

RELISHES
Stuffed Celery—Glace .... $ .75
Green Olives—Glace .... .85
Rose Radishes—Glace .... .50
Italian Pepperonis .... .50
Heart of Pascal Celery—Glace .... .50
Young Green Onions—Glace .... .50
Ripe Olives—Glace .... .50
Carrot Sticks—Glace .... .50

CHEESE PLATE
Imp. Roquefort .... .75
Dom. Roquefort .... .50 Camembert .... .50
Served With Ritz Crackers

SPECIAL APPETIZERS
Hors d'Oeuvre Plate 1.50
Anchovy, au Roi 1.00
Pickled Shrimp de'Elmo 1.00
Pickled Marinated Herring .... .75
Caviar Canapes .... .75
Anchovy Canapes .... .75
Marinated Artichokes .... .85

SAUCES
Mushroom Sauce .... .50 Spanish .... .50
Sauce Bereau .... .75 Bob Special Sauce .... .50

SALADS
Pineapple and Cottage Cheese Salad 1.50
Lobster 1.25
Sea Food Salad 1.00
Crab 1.00
Shrimp 1.00
Tuna .... .80
Asparagus Tips .... .75
Lettuce and Tomato .... .75
Grapefruit Salad .... .85
Combination .... .85
Heart of Lettuce .... .50
Avocado Stuffed with Crabmeat 2.50

Imported Italian Antipasto $1.50
Flaming Shrimp Cocktail $1.00

Appetizers and Cocktails

Large Fresh Jumbo Shrimp Cocktail $1.00
Lobster Meat Cocktail 1.00
Crabmeat Cocktail .... .85
Blue Points Cocktail (in season) .... .85
Shrimp Cocktail .... .75
Oyster Cocktail .... .75
Pineapple-Frappe .... .85
Seafood Cocktail .... .85
Tomato Juice-Frappe .... .50
Grapefruit Supreme .... .50

and then make his one foot taller. The sign beckoned customers to come to his club that was "The Talk of the Town" with "No Cover Charge Any time."

His son, Mike Porter, who viewed his father as "a mountain of respect," described the neon sign as having one huge hand waving to greet, while the thumb of the other hand directed customers in toward his club. The sign was not only seen from the ground, Mike reported, but "the pilots at the airport used Dad's sign as a kind of beacon or lighthouse when coming into Billings from the southwest." He continued, "The sign had about twelve DC motors that ran both arms. At the time, it cost about $300 per month to keep the sign on and operating twenty-four hours a day, except the neon lights came on at night via a timer."

Sunday dinner at the Elmo Club started at 4:00 p.m., with choices of "lake trout, tender steaks, golden chicken, cool salads, sea foods and Italian dishes." On Monday evenings, champagne happy hours provided more festivities. Music began at 9:00 p.m., with Porter bringing in names such as Joe Darby and his seven-piece Society Orchestra, Dale Hall (the exotic black-light dancer), Mack Malone and Sharon performing the floorshow "Summer Revue" and Jack Kerns with his six-piece band.

Elmo Club plate, late 1940s. *Courtesy of James M. Reich.*

For food, Porter's menu ranged from meatballs and spaghetti for $2 a plate, to Chinese dishes, to steaks and seafood, including lobster thermidor for $3.25 and Louisiana frog legs with tartar sauce for the same price, pan-fried chicken and steak, including Chateaubriand with Sauce Bereau for $9. The Elmo Club bragged about its Chinese food, with the following notes under the header with selections of "Sweet and Sour Ribs and Noodles": "We are particularly proud of our Chinese Cuisine...the reason will be obvious once you have tried it." Unfortunately, the gratification ended on the last morning in April 1961, when the second Elmo Club burned down. This time the estimated damage was $75,000, and only a small portion was covered by insurance.

In 1952, Porter purchased the Turf Club in downtown Billings from Maurice B. Egan. From there, he supplied a shuttle to his Elmo Club on Laurel Road. At the Turf Club, he started the Porterhouse lounge in the back of the Turf Bar. As it was conveniently located across the alley from the *Billings Gazette*, he shrewdly courted newspaper people, who made his place their unofficial headquarters. The first press club in Billings met there. The name of his lounge originated not from the steaks served at the club but from the *Gazette* staff who long before had called the owner "Porterhouse Bob." Mike Porter believed there actually was "a feud between the *Gazette* and my dad." Whenever there was a violation, his father made front-page news. Mike added, "The *Gazette* was a thorn in my father's side."

Mostly, Porter prided himself on beating the system. In his obituary, a newsman friend who had reported on Porter's brushes with the law said, "Most kids love playing cops and robbers but then grow up to forget about it. This is one part of Bob that never grew up. He still gets more kick out of making a buck on the thin edge of the law than most guys do making 10 by staying well on the safe side."

"The police was always raiding the Turf because Dad always served drinks after 2:00 a.m.," Mike Porter said. He knew of the violations because he worked as a dishwasher in his high school years starting in 1968 and was often at the Turf Club after the time cutoff for alcohol sales and gambling. "Dad had no diplomacy. He put that on my mother." Throughout fifty years of marriage, Mike's mother, Elizabeth "Betty" Hanna Fletcher, softened her husband's behavior.

On December 17, 1950, Porter was charged with selling drinks after closing hours. Then on April 30, 1970, police raided the Turf Nite Spot. The storm netted 460 punch boards, a dice table, dice and other gambling equipment, all of which led to Porter's and bartender Dennis Willits's arrests.

Once again a Porter enterprise smoldered to the ground on Saturday, August 14, 1971. The fire that leveled the Turf, located at 14 North Twenty-seventh Street, was believed to have started in the kitchen where a cook was broiling potatoes and meat. According to Fire Chief Curtis Magruder, "It looks like there was a little delay in calling the fire department, but we are trying to determine how long the delay may have been." This was one of the largest downtown fires the department had seen in years.

After the Turf Club burned down, Porter left the restaurant and bar business to run the Big Sky Campground on the site of his Elmo Club on Laurel Road until his health failed and he passed away in 1993.

Lake Elmo Club: Annual Music Party, May 6, 1955

On May 6, 1955, Allan Downs, an amateur filmmaker, recorded the musician party held at the Lake Elmo Club on Laurel Road.

Downs, a chiropractor by day and a jazz buff by night, recorded flickering images of the bigger-than-life neon sign waving musicians and their guests into the club for an "afternoon of hilarity and good music." On this clear and windy day, Chevys packed the parking lot edged with small piles of snow. Presumably, Downs provided the lighthearted narration, admitting he arrived at 2:30 p.m., when the main dining room was "buzzing with activity" by the time the crew arrived. "Standing room only, partner, and no WCTU members allowed," Downs jokingly alluded to the Woman's Christian Temperance Union, which helped establish the Eighteenth Amendment putting a ban on alcohol.

The guests at the Elmo Club that afternoon seemed to tolerate Downs's presence with the lights and camera. The women seemed most annoyed that their lives were being recorded. The lights irritated more than inspired in the dim-lit club, with Downs commenting, "The Elmo swallowed light up like it was a stranger." Cold shoulders and camera shyness showed in Downs' Club 1011 Pictures. Even Della Mae Logan, Billings' most famous madam, "was wishing the camera would go home." But in other cases, "some, shall we say were too busy to notice. It was a shame to throw so much light on so many loving couples. This was the sort of afternoon where you start by shaking hands and then end up rubbing necks to alleviate nervous tension."

Patrons sported their best fashion, with men in ties and shawl-collared jackets with low buttoning and low-placed pockets or double-breasted jackets. Women, with short cropped haircuts sporting waves and curls, wore shin-length dresses with flared skirts pinched at the waist. Stilettos, peep-toes and platform-style shoes mimicking screen goddesses like Marilyn Monroe and Grace Kelly enhanced dance moves. High collars, scarves around the neck, cropped cardigans, hats and fur stoles accessorized the feminine dress.

The big band that highlighted the afternoon included Johnny Peterson, Joe Story and Russ Davies dressed in black jackets playing clarinets, saxophones, trumpets and drums. Guests filled the dance floor, swaying to the beat. Later, the Midway changed the tone and mood with snappy drumbeat music played by men wearing plaid shirts and western bow ties. The music moved from brass to wood with guitar, bass and violin music inspiring twirling dance steps. The Skyliners brought more big-city jazz. An all-black band with men in double-breasted suits and a female pianist played "Shake, Rattle and Roll." Downs said of the dancers, "To each his own dance step. It is as many different styles as you would care to notice."

Abundant food buffets set on long tables lined with white tablecloths provided generous offerings. Large silver platters brimmed with what appeared to be sliced cold cuts and cheese, green salads with cherry tomatoes and steak and potatoes. The camera captured the chef—dressed in white with a puffy chef hat tilted to the side—grilling steaks. Downs commented, "If you enjoy your steak dinner, extend your appreciation to the Elmo Club chef. He's got three of those small steers on the grill now." On the abundance of the offerings, he said, "Trying to make a dent in the buffet was like trying to get ahead of the distillery, the food just kept coming and coming."

At times, the wait for a drink from a white-shirted bartender was "three deep." Oval mirrors behind the bar reflected the making of the Prairie Martini, which Downs described as "straight formaldehyde with a spider riding on the olive."

The film ends with the bold letters "THE END," capturing an era after World War II with the influx of the American cinema and television along with the new beat of rock-and-roll. The closing of Bob Porter's Elmo Club ended an era of "hilarity and good music."

The Skyline Club

The Skyline Club was originally the home of Mr. and Mrs. Charles O. Myers and their eleven children. Between 1913 and 1917, with the help of stonemasons, they built their house on top of the Rims. Myers and his sons

The Charles O. Myers home was converted to the Skyline Club in 1944. Later, it took on the name of the Bella Vista Club. *Courtesy of Stella Fong.*

carved a set of steps into the Rims at the current Arvin Lane so the younger children could get to school. Metal posts still mark where the steps were. Later, they built what has become known as Myers Trail, allowing Myers to drive his car home.

When the twenty-eight-room home was completed, it had a ballroom, twelve bedrooms and two dining rooms. Family members eventually left home or died, and the residence finally became vacant in 1944. Two years later, architect William Reid decided the site was ideal for a nightclub. The building was then modernized and operated as a nightclub by Bert Redeau of Casper, Wyoming, and Wes Hughes of Cascade, Montana. Even though they brought in big-name entertainment such as Al Overend and his Society Orchestra and hosted the annual Billings Local No. 439 of the Musicians Union annual banquet, they never prospered.

While in operation, the venue, a "Mile West of the Airport Top of the Rims," offered a place for dances, reunions, weddings and other gatherings. Examples of happenings included the Billings Alumni Association of Sigma Alpha Epsilon holding a semi-formal dance for fifty people, the Montana Motor Transport auxiliary meeting for a dessert luncheon and the Montana Sigma Chi members hosting a luncheon and smoker. Food offerings ranged from a special turkey dinner with all the trimmings for Thanksgiving 1948 to a Smorgasbord Dinner Dance on Sunday nights in 1949 for two dollars with an all-you-can-eat buffet of seven entree choices.

At the end of 1956, Mike and Rita Basile, who ran the old Midway Club, bought the Skyline Club, operating it for nine years. They renamed the club the Bella Vista (Beautiful View) Club and served Italian and American dinners under "Mike Basile's personal supervision." Pete Zagorda—who frequented the club with his wife, Doris—remembered dancing to Bill Vitt and his five-piece band and listening to Kay Cahill play piano music. But Zagorda's biggest and proudest memory was how his grandmother Arcangalina Cucciardi, the eldest of three sisters, taught Mike Basile how to cook the spaghetti sauce that continued to be served at the Bella Vista Club.

Chuck Hauptman believed the main reason his wife, Anne, married him was because "I was such a great dancer." Hauptman, a geologist, and his wife relocated to Billings in the early 1950s, and he was one of the original founders of the Petroleum Club. He clearly remembered going to the Bella Vista on August 17, 1959, with the "ladies all dressed up." After an evening of dining and dancing with friends, they drove down from the Rims to head home. At 11:36 p.m., Hauptman thought he had too much to drink, as the car appeared to move out of control. Hauptman was actually experiencing a magnitude-7.5 earthquake that had just struck northwest of Yellowstone National Park, near Hebgen Lake. Its intensity was felt clear to Billings.

In 1965, after her husband's death, Rita Basile sold the club to the Great Plains Life Insurance Co. A group from Casper, Wyoming, then formed Skyline Club Inc. and took over the club about two years later. This group proposed the construction of a motel complex but faced much opposition from the community. The Eastern Montana College Wilderness Club collected three thousand signatures petitioning a delay in the construction, as they wanted an investigation into alternatives in commercial development.

On the Fourth of July in 1971, the club burned down. Bob Henry, operator and part owner, estimated the building's worth to be $200,000 to $300,000. The fire department arrived with two trucks, a pumper and an aerial ladder, as officers believed someone was trapped on the upper level of the three-story building. The Billings Fire Department left the site because it thought it had been falsely called. Since the building was located outside the city limits and the club had not subscribed to the private O'Donnell's Fire Service serving the area, the building was lost, and "the once fashionable supper club looked like a Druid burial ground." According to Addison Bragg, the "wannabe club managers" who were staging a hard rock concert at the Skyline Club ended up with the club burning down. At the time, Henry believed the group would rebuild.

The Windmill Club

In the 1930s, Toots Maybell opened the Windmill Club on First Avenue South. The Windmill Club was primarily a dance club serving beer and wine. Toots sold the business to Ralph Studer, who sold the club to Louis and Muggs Eastman in 1940. Louis and Muggs remodeled the interior and began a full-service menu in 1947, seating up to sixty-five customers.

The Eastmans ran $1.50 specials with service after 5:00 p.m. for the "Famous Windmill Foods" consisting of Louisiana prawns in sweet and sour sauce, sirloin steak in a basket, barbecue Missouri spareribs and fried chicken, Windmill style. They advertised drinks "Mixed the Way You Want 'em!" and brought in attractions such as Bill Dixon with his song stories and piano presentations.

In 1965, after remodeling and enlarging the club, they recruited the "Culinary Talents" of Chef Eldon K. Dovich from Diamond Jim's in

Minneapolis. Meals always began with a crudité tray featuring carrots, celery, pickles and olives. Aside from steak, the Windmill signature dishes included king crab legs and a pile of shrimp eaten with a plastic bib. Jeanne Moller remembered that when she was a girl, "unless you were in a booth you were sitting inches from the next table. The place was dark and intimate. Growing up, that was the place we got to go because chicken in a basket was five dollars. You could have a hamburger and chicken in a basket. There were six of us."

In the early '80s, John and Scottie Novasio bought the Windmill Club. In his twenty-two years operating the business, John made one major change: he got rid of the iconic red-and-white checkered tablecloths. He did not change the menu, though he did raise the prices. Novasio said, "I have never charged a customer for a cup of coffee." Throughout the years, the restaurant continued to be famous for its baby fist–sized shrimp.

Novasio also did not alter the not-so-convenient ladies' room. With just one toilet, the Eastmans knew they needed to expand the restroom. In order to fit in another toilet, they built it so that a woman had to go through one stall to get to the other one. A wood-colored accordion door separated the two. Kenny Roesch, who worked at the Windmill as a busboy during this period, thought the women's restroom was "bizarre." While "many of the women were quite horrified," they knew when nature called one no longer cared.

The front door held a speakeasy peephole that allowed for selection of who could join in the festivities inside the Windmill. After all the Billings bars officially closed at 2:00 a.m., people arrived at the Windmill and hoped to pass inspection at the peephole. Many stayed into the wee hours of the morning, and supposedly steak and eggs were offered, drowned by cocktails.

Roesch recalled people packing the Windmill for food right after the bars closed: "There was not a restaurant in town that was open in the morning." The patrons would "finally filter out and then the bar would open at 3:30 to 4:00 in the morning for any friends, family or employees. The busboys would always be bartenders. You learn how to make whiskey and Coke, vodka and 7Up."

At year's end in 2005, the Novasios closed the club on First Avenue South, seeking retirement. But Don Bottrell, a longtime Windmill customer, collaborated with the Novasios to re-create the Windmill in an 8,400-square-foot restaurant in the West End on Trans Tech Way. The larger space removed the intimacy of the old place. It highlighted a cathedral ceiling bearing timber beams above large double sandstone gas fireplaces. Today, the patio with a view of a two-acre pond brimming with wildlife and ten-foot-long fire pit is a new popular gathering place.

The Billings Petroleum Club

The Billings Petroleum Club began with the informal gathering of men in the oil business in the Northern Hotel in the early 1950s. The group incorporated on April 16, 1954, during the early boom years of the oil industry in Montana and Wyoming. The club headquarters settled in a vacant building adjacent to the Stockman Bar and Cafe, with a contract negotiated with Stockman's owners, Les Fischbach and Lou Hall.

By mid-year 1959, major oil companies and larger independents were moving out of Billings as production fell, hurting the membership in the club. President Darrell Black, Shell Oil Company landman, led an effort to save the club. The club decided it needed a more attractive meeting place with outstanding cuisine and service and support of the downtown businesses.

On November 27, 1959, the Petroleum Club joined with the Northern Hotel to build a two-story annex. The club signed a fifteen-year lease to occupy the basement and ground floor of the hotel. In June 1960, the Petroleum Club moved in. A small group of businessmen called the "Sheepherders" recommended that the association ask volunteers to prepay their dues for the fifteen-year life of the lease so the proceeds could be used to fund capital improvements.

In September 1977, the club was approached by architect and businessman Harrison Fagg about relocating to the top floor of a proposed eighteen-story Sheraton Hotel. The Sheraton was to replace an old livery stable owned by Fagg's family that had been severely damaged in a fire. A year later, when approval for the building occurred, it was to be a twenty-two-story hotel. Just short of the Petroleum Club's twenty-seventh anniversary, on January 2, 1981, it settled into the highest floor of the 305-room hotel that cost $13 million to build. For four years, it was the tallest building in Billings, until the 255-foot-tall First Interstate Tower was erected.

By the fall of 2002, the club was struggling to keep the membership alive, so it assumed the name of Billings Professional Club. Before the group had to liquidate its assets, members stepped up with financing toward a five-year loan, with plans to make changes in operation and service. A survey of the members in 2003 demonstrated a preference for the club to restore the name Billings Petroleum Club.

In 2004, Lance Johnson took the helm in the Petroleum Club kitchen after eighteen years at the Hilands Golf Club. Johnson had earned an art and art education degree from Montana State University–Billings working under Ben Steele and John Pollock. To pay for college, he worked part time as a dishwasher at the Hilands Golf Club, which eventually turned into his becoming the chef. When not cooking, he honed his skills as a watercolor and oil painter. As a chef, Johnson became most famous for his ice sculptures. With chainsaw and pick, he created many waist-high creations, from hearts to swans for weddings and two dolphins breaching straight upward to a grand piano.

In 2014, Johnson walked away from the food business to pursue his love of painting. The years he spent fishing and hiking in the Montana wilderness led him to paint Big Sky landscapes, native works and wildlife. These days, he co-owns Sunrise Studio and Art Gallery at 2923 Montana Avenue.

Other Clubs

In the late 1940s and through the 1950s, the Beacon, Midway, Billings and Vegas Clubs kept fingers snapping, heads bobbing and toes tapping. The Vegas Club operated for nearly twenty years on First Avenue North and Twenty-fifth Street until it burned down with an estimated $100,000 in damage on December 21, 1976. As the club burned, loyal customers and employees lined the sidewalks outside the scene and cried. The Vegas Club originally opened in the 1940s, when it was purchased by Ottelia "Toots" Woods. When Woods died in 1958, her widower managed the business until Mr. and Mrs. Maurice B. Egan purchased the club during the week of October 5, 1959. The Egans vowed to continue the food specialties of the house and the businessman's luncheons popularized by Mrs. Woods.

In 1947, the Egans remodeled the Vegas Club with Lamb's, a bar and restaurant and supplies business, which resulted in "colorful surroundings." From a jukebox on the back wall, music pulsed around the curved bar flanked with metal ringed stools and through the round booths. Advertisements for the club depicted the cartoon character Bubbles, who was depicted as blond and buxom. She gave the club a flirtatious vibe, yet ads purported "pleasant, harmonious surroundings" and a place where "we streamlined things so that your order is at your elbow, muy pronto!"

When Toots Woods was operating the club in 1957, shipments of "peak-of-the-season sea foods" came in on Fridays, so fresh clams, "oysters en Half-shell, Dungeness Crab, Jumbo Frog Legs and African Lobster Tail" were "Prepared and served the Vegas Club way!" along with "Vegas Club Prime Steaks."

The Midway Club at 209 North Fourteenth Street provided "Smart Dancing, Outstanding Foods" and "Smooth Drinks." There, "Your Pleasure is our Command!" Woods also owned the Billings Club, where "Northern Appetites Respond to Wonderful Southern Foods." Along with banquet and luncheon facilities, music with "Sultry, Deep-South Tunes by Dick Fio Rito's Band" played as "Tall, Cold Drinks" were served.

The Beacon Club, located at the junction of Main Street and Lake Elmo, was "the Fun spot of Billings." For dancing pleasure, the club's entertainment included "Danny Morris and his Fine Band…Bob Mann, Chuck Mulken, Eddie Neibauer, and Sammy Fiske…featuring harmony singing, special vocal numbers, and the best dance music in the Midland Empire. Don't forget Buster at the piano! As Danny says, 'The man with 40 fingers.'" In the kitchen, Sparky or Dorothy did the cooking. In the summer of 1951, Harold and Pat Kinsey announced their association with the Beacon Club.

With dinner specials for two dollars on February 24, 1957, the Beacon Club hosted "America's foremost female impersonators! Carroll Wallace, the world's most beautiful boy and Jackie Phillips, the female Jerry Lewis. Positively the funniest act ever booked anywhere!" headlined the entertainment. Owner Syd Thomas and Chef Bill Borner definitely brought color to the Magic City.

In the beginning of 1963, Joe and Kay Koory, who had their own piano and drum act, became the new owners and operators of the Beacon Club and renamed it Koory's Beacon Club. Ray Price and his Cherokee Cowboy Band topped their first lineups as the new proprietors. Alongside artists such as Bob Rogge Quintet, the Koorys offered ladies' night with style shows to fulfill their mantra: "If It's Fun You're Seekin'…Head for the Beacon."

On the night of September 17, 1947, the Billings Club had "Mammy Night" featuring "Southern Style Foods Perfectly Prepared!…Properly Served!" On this night, the menu started with "Stuffed Celery Sticks—Cottage Cheese Salad, Cream of Asparagus Soup." Entrees included "½ Spring Chicken on Toast for $1.60, Prime Ribs of 4-H Beef au jus for $2.00, Grilled Chicken Livers with Bacon Strips for $1.75." Items priced around $3.00 included filet mignon, French fried scallops and fresh eastern oysters. "Hot Rolls, Fresh Fruit Jello or Bleu Cheese" finished the meal. Larry Lyons' Band entertained with "Smooth Music." Less than a week later, the Billings Club was serving up "Deliciously Fresh" seafood, steaks and chicken, as well as the exotic offering of frog legs.

The Stock Exchange

In the late 1970s, Sam McDonald and James Corning opened the Stock Exchange Bar, Restaurant and Disco at 1000 First Avenue North. Corning asked his son, Steve, to return to Billings, his boyhood home, from Los Angeles to manage the new enterprise. According to the younger Corning, his father and McDonald, after countless trips to Denver, decided to open a fancy steak restaurant with a bar and disco. Many dollars were spent in remodeling the old Pierce Packing Chicken House. Steve Corning returned from California in 1979 as the discotheque was struggling and surmised that "they probably over capitalized for the scope of the market at the time. Neither one of them had experience with the food business."

With the help of Corby Skinner, the dance venue in the basement of the building became known as the Prairie based on the popularity of the movie *Urban Cowboy*. Cloth covered the walls in colors that mimicked the sunset on the prairie. Skinner told of how they painted fluorescent dots that sparkled like stars in the late evening. The dance floor took up the center of the room, with benches placed along the walls. A large, wraparound bar looked onto the dance floor and then to the DJ booth. Waitresses in cowboy vests, mini skirts and boots served the Long Island iced teas, Harvey Wallbangers and grasshoppers.

Upstairs, the restaurant took on the air of the old railroad dining room, with chandeliers and wainscoting packaged in floral-striped ornate wallpaper. Queen back chairs were tucked under heavy wooden tables that were draped with white tablecloths. Skinner remembered rooms in colors of burgundy and green. Waiters, uniformed in white shirts and leather vests, tossed the tableside Caesar salads with lemon juice squeezed from lemons wrapped in cheesecloth. They delivered what "everyone got—the shrimp boat on ice," according to Skinner. Steve Corning described the Stock Exchange as "the typical steak, crab leg kind of restaurant. Cocktail shrimp. Prime rib."

In November 1980, Bess Snyder returned home to Billings from Los Angeles to stay with friends. While she was home alone, John Fredlund showed up at the door with pheasants he had hunted that day. Not knowing how to prepare the birds, John took Bess out to dinner and then drinks at the Stock Exchange afterward. Bess recalled, "There was a slide that led from the restaurant/bar to the disco located in the basement. Although the disco was closed for the night, we got permission to check it out. Once we figured out how to turn on the lights, we cranked up the music and danced for about an hour." Two months later, John asked for Bess's hand in marriage.

Upon entering the Stock Exchange through the circular doors, guests were ensconced in what Skinner described as "an old hotel lobby feel." From here, guests could step down the stairs to the Prairie or head up a few steps to the restaurant with a bar on one side and the restaurant on the other. From the bar, there was a metal slide that swooshed patrons down to the disco.

"We had people waiting at the door to get in," Skinner continued. "The Stock Exchange was a huge college hangout." Fashion shows—with

The Stock Exchange today. The Pierce Packing Chicken House was home to the Stock Exchange Restaurant, Bar and Disco in the late 1970s and Bruno's Italian Restaurant in the early 2000s. *Courtesy of Stella Fong.*

The original slide from the Stock Exchange, gliding clients down to the Prairie Disco. *Courtesy of Stella Fong.*

cheerleaders and basketball players from Eastern Montana College as models—were popular. Also, Skinner taught everyone the line dance the Wanderer, only to wind down the night with Frank Sinatra to "mellow people out to get them out the door."

Steve Corning admitted, "For two years we did it. It was putting on a party every night." The Stock Exchange was where "everyone was young and part of the party. It became the center of gravity for nightlife…You become this completely nocturnal creature." The younger Corning left the business in 1981, and it continued until 1984 with a manager.

In the early 1990s, Mike and Toni Sammartino took over the building with their restaurant Bruno's, A Taste of Italy. For about six years, they ran their restaurant out of this building. Mike said, "We lasted longer than Corning and McDonald." They spent $150,000 to remodel the space in the basement to accommodate special events and banquets with a catering kitchen. In the twenty-seven years the Sammartinos were in business, Bruno's served their grandmother Rita Basile's recipes for cavatelli, chicken ravioli and gnocchi, all made from scratch. The Sammartinos established Bruno's in several locations, selling their last place of business at 1911 King Avenue on June 1, 2015, to Darla Hartung. They liquidated their house and shortly thereafter moved to Honduras to escape the Billings winters.

With a soft luster of perspiration on her brow, she glanced at the car's side-view mirror on her ride home. She began her evening before stepping out the door by checking her lipstick. Through the years, pink evolved to red and then black and fashions changed from flared dresses to flared bell bottoms and double-breasted suits to jump suits. The Magic City clubs—Elmo, Skyline, the Stock Exchange and more—heightened taste buds and heartbeats.

4

THE LUZON CAFE

The Leading and Most Popular Café in Billings

In 1927, an advertisement in the *Billings Gazette* once again touted the Luzon Cafe's slogan: "The Leading and Most Popular Cafe in Billings, 44 years of Faithful Service." The café had been recently remodeled by "adding a banquet room that will accommodate 60 persons more." But the secret to better food was the installation of York Sanitary Refrigeration.

Located at 2711 Montana Avenue, this was "a home of good food and features cleanliness, quality and service—a favorite place for people from the territory for many miles around—specialize in Oriental dishes, lunches, dinners and Sunday d'hote dinners." The establishment had a soda fountain and served the "best of food." Supposedly, there was "not a more attractively furnished restaurant in this part of the state" and no other place that had "attained a greater measure of popularity." An eight-course table d'Hote included a turkey and fried chicken dinner for the special price of one dollar.

In 1883, the Luzon Cafe was the original location for a trading post called the Delmonico. "But when a Chinaman from the Philippines took over the following year and started a hamburger stand, he named it Luzon when very few residents knew or cared that Luzon was the name of the large southern island of the Philippines." According to Joe Fava, the owner in 1948, some of the distinguished stockmen who had patronized the café included Charlie Baers, Eddie and Jack Frazier, John Ross and John D. Losecamp.

The property, originally owned by the Minnesota and Montana Land and Improvement Company, was transferred to Elise N. Mund in 1884. It was believed that the first building, built in 1884, was used for a restaurant

Luzon Cafe on Montana Avenue, 1920s. *Courtesy of the Western Heritage Center.*

A serving dish and sugar bowl from the Luzon Cafe. *Courtesy of James M. Reich.*

by Van Loon and Hanson until 1887. A year later, Harry Cross ran the establishment, only to have it taken over by J.W. Vaughn and, later, his brother George, with the restaurant taking on the name of Vaughn's

8-10-13

-DINNER MENU-

-SERVED FROM 11;30 A.M. TILL OUT-

SOUP--Puree of Chicken Giblet--------------------10¢

-RELISHES-

Sliced Tomatoes----------25¢ Young Radishes------15¢
Sliced Cucumbers--------25¢ Young Oni8ns-------15¢
Dressed Lettuce--------25¢ Stuffed Mangoes--15¢

-FISH-

Boiled Salt Mackerel, Boiled Potatoes------------50¢
Fried Halibut Steak, Maitre D' Hotel------------40¢
Grilled Lake Trout, Butter Sauce----------------50¢

-READY TO SERVE-

Boiled Ox Tongue, Spanish---------------------------40¢
Fricassee of Chicken, Green Peas-----------------50¢
Braised Sirloin of Beef with Noodles-------------40¢
Pork Tenderloin Saute, Mushrooms-----------------50¢
HOT ROAST BEEF SANDWICH WITH COFFEE-----------25¢

-TO ORDER-

1/2 Spring Chicken on Toast, Cream Gravy----------65¢
Chipped Beef Scrambled with Ranch Eggs-----------40¢
Grilled Mutton Chops, Rasher of Bacon------------50¢
Calf's Liver Saute, Plain------------------------35¢
Corn Beef Hash, Poached Egg-------------------40¢
Home-Made Sausage, Country Gravy-------------40¢
Veal Chops, Hunter's Style------------------50¢
Van Camp's Pork & Beans-------------------35¢
Sirloin Steak, A La Colonial--------------60¢
Cheese Omelet---------------------------------50¢

-ROASTS-

Roast Leg of Fresh Pork, Brown Gravy---------------40¢
Roast Prime Ribs of Beef Au Jus--------------------40¢
EXTRA CUT--50¢

-VEGETABLES-

Mashed or Steamed Potatoes--------------------------10¢
Asparagus on Cream---20¢ Corn on the Cob--------10¢

-DESSERTS-

Iced Watermelon---20¢
1/2 Iced Cantaloupe---15¢ Whole-----------------25¢
Raspberries & Cream--25¢ Peaches & Cream-----15¢
Apple Pie A La Mode-----------------------------------20¢
Chocolate or Cocoanut Cake Per Cut-------------10¢
Lemon, Pumpkin, Custard, Apple & Raisin Pies------10¢
ICE CREAM AND CAKE------------------------------------15¢
Free with Dinner Orders from 11;30 A.M. to 5:00 P.M.

A typewritten dinner menu from Luzon Cafe, August 10, 1913. *Courtesy of James M. Reich.*

Restaurant. A later enlargement included the Vienna Bakery. In 1898, Lon Quock and Joseph Parque bought the restaurant and renamed it the Delmonico. Parque was one of Billings' first milkmen, with a farm a short distance east of town. Unfortunately, the Delmonico failed and was sold in 1901 to James McCune, who had operated the Northern Pacific lunch counter. He renamed the establishment the Metropolitan. In 1903, Ogburn and Kell took over the business for six years only to later sell to D.O. Jackson and George Helm. Clarence F. Wood, who stepped off a westbound train in 1906 and crossed the muddy streets, recalled, "I went down to the Luzon Cafe and got the scare of my life. The place was filled with rough looking cowboys and sheepherders."

The cover of the Luzon Cafe menu from 1943. *Courtesy of James M. Reich.*

Jackson later sold his interest to Mrs. Frank Boyd in 1910, and she ran the business with Helm until 1917. According to Miss Melville Moss, a Red Cross worker, food was prepared at the Luzon Cafe and brought to the depot for service for the World War I troops coming through Billings on the train on January 24, 1919. In 1919, Luzon Cafe changed hands again as Boyd transferred the business to Jack Pappas and Gus Fetros, who "remodeled, renovated, redecorated and enlarged several times, always in response to the greater demands made by the public for Luzon service."

On February 19, 1931, the Luzon Cafe presented its new Persian Garden. On that night, beginning at six o'clock, Val Bisonette's Orchestra played in the dining and dancing space "where everyone will be happy." Persian Garden came to be because of the owners' travels through the eastern states and Europe. "Having viewed the

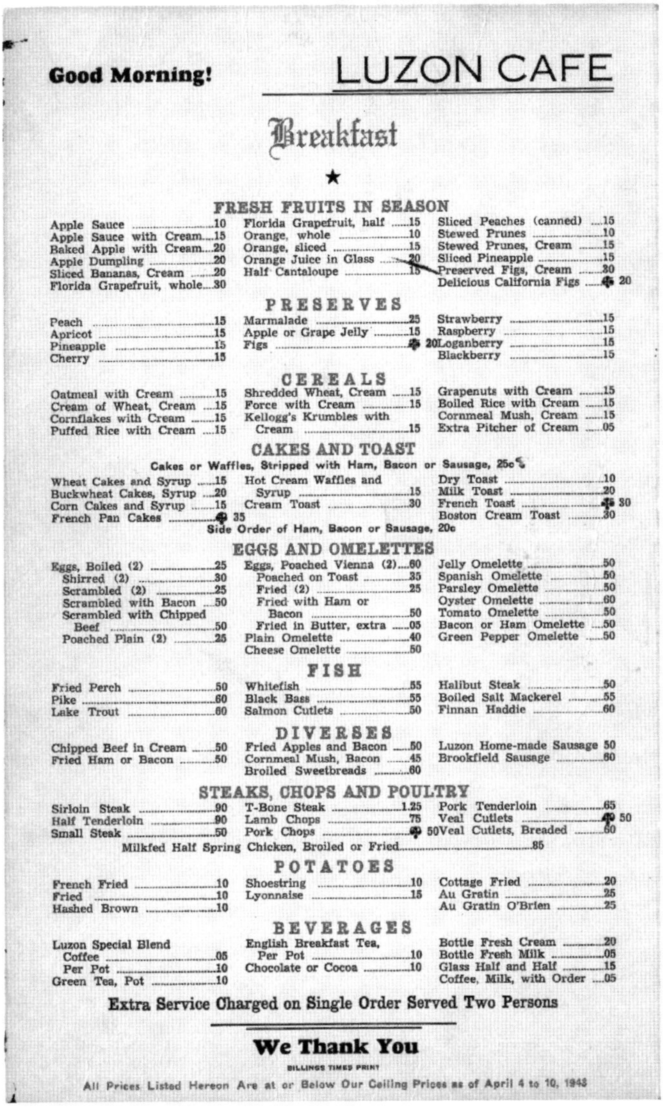

Good Morning!

LUZON CAFE

Breakfast

★

FRESH FRUITS IN SEASON

Apple Sauce .... .10
Apple Sauce with Cream .... .15
Baked Apple with Cream .... .20
Apple Dumpling .... .20
Sliced Bananas, Cream .... .20
Florida Grapefruit, whole .... .30
Florida Grapefruit, half .... .15
Orange, whole .... .10
Orange, sliced .... .15
Orange Juice in Glass .... .20
Half Cantaloupe .... .15
Sliced Peaches (canned) .... .15
Stewed Prunes .... .10
Stewed Prunes, Cream .... .15
Sliced Pineapple .... .15
Preserved Figs, Cream .... .30
Delicious California Figs 20

PRESERVES

Peach .... .15
Apricot .... .15
Pineapple .... .15
Cherry .... .15
Marmalade .... .25
Apple or Grape Jelly .... .15
Figs 20
Strawberry .... .15
Raspberry .... .15
Loganberry .... .15
Blackberry .... .15

CEREALS

Oatmeal with Cream .... .15
Cream of Wheat, Cream .... .15
Cornflakes with Cream .... .15
Puffed Rice with Cream .... .15
Shredded Wheat, Cream .... .15
Force with Cream .... .15
Kellogg's Krumbles with Cream .... .15
Grapenuts with Cream .... .15
Boiled Rice with Cream .... .15
Cornmeal Mush, Cream .... .15
Extra Pitcher of Cream .... .05

CAKES AND TOAST

Cakes or Waffles, Stripped with Ham, Bacon or Sausage, 25c

Wheat Cakes and Syrup .... .15
Buckwheat Cakes, Syrup .... .20
Corn Cakes and Syrup .... .15
French Pan Cakes 35
Hot Cream Waffles and Syrup .... .15
Cream Toast .... .30
Dry Toast .... .10
Milk Toast .... .20
French Toast 30
Boston Cream Toast .... .30

Side Order of Ham, Bacon or Sausage, 20c

EGGS AND OMELETTES

Eggs, Boiled (2) .... .25
Shirred (2) .... .30
Scrambled (2) .... .25
Scrambled with Bacon .... .50
Scrambled with Chipped Beef .... .50
Poached Plain (2) .... .25
Eggs, Poached Vienna (2) .... .60
Poached on Toast .... .35
Fried (2) .... .25
Fried with Ham or Bacon .... .50
Fried in Butter, extra .... .05
Plain Omelette .... .40
Cheese Omelette .... .50
Jelly Omelette .... .50
Spanish Omelette .... .50
Parsley Omelette .... .50
Oyster Omelette .... .60
Tomato Omelette .... .50
Bacon or Ham Omelette .... .50
Green Pepper Omelette .... .50

FISH

Fried Perch .... .50
Pike .... .60
Lake Trout .... .60
Whitefish .... .55
Black Bass .... .55
Salmon Cutlets .... .50
Halibut Steak .... .50
Boiled Salt Mackerel .... .55
Finnan Haddie .... .60

DIVERSES

Chipped Beef in Cream .... .50
Fried Ham or Bacon .... .50
Fried Apples and Bacon .... .50
Cornmeal Mush, Bacon .... .45
Broiled Sweetbreads .... .60
Luzon Home-made Sausage 50
Brookfield Sausage .... .60

STEAKS, CHOPS AND POULTRY

Sirloin Steak .... .90
Half Tenderloin .... .90
Small Steak .... .50
T-Bone Steak 1.25
Lamb Chops .... .75
Pork Chops 50
Pork Tenderloin .... .65
Veal Cutlets 50
Veal Cutlets, Breaded .... .60

Milkfed Half Spring Chicken, Broiled or Fried .... .85

POTATOES

French Fried .... .10
Fried .... .10
Hashed Brown .... .10
Shoestring .... .10
Lyonnaise .... .15
Cottage Fried .... .20
Au Gratin .... .25
Au Gratin O'Brien .... .25

BEVERAGES

Luzon Special Blend Coffee .... .05
Per Pot .... .10
Green Tea, Pot .... .10
English Breakfast Tea, Per Pot .... .10
Chocolate or Cocoa .... .10
Bottle Fresh Cream .... .20
Bottle Fresh Milk .... .05
Glass Half and Half .... .15
Coffee, Milk, with Order .... .05

Extra Service Charged on Single Order Served Two Persons

We Thank You

BILLINGS TIMES PRINT

All Prices Listed Hereon Are at or Below Our Ceiling Prices as of April 4 to 10, 1943

The inside of the menu from Luzon Cafe with advertising. *Courtesy of James M. Reich.*

beautiful cafés and dining places in foreign lands, the management of the Luzon was imbibed with the desire to open such a place for the amusement loving public of the Midland Empire." On January 18, 1932, the café was slightly damaged by an electrical fire originating from an electric piano. "A short circuit caused the blaze, which was extinguished with chemicals."

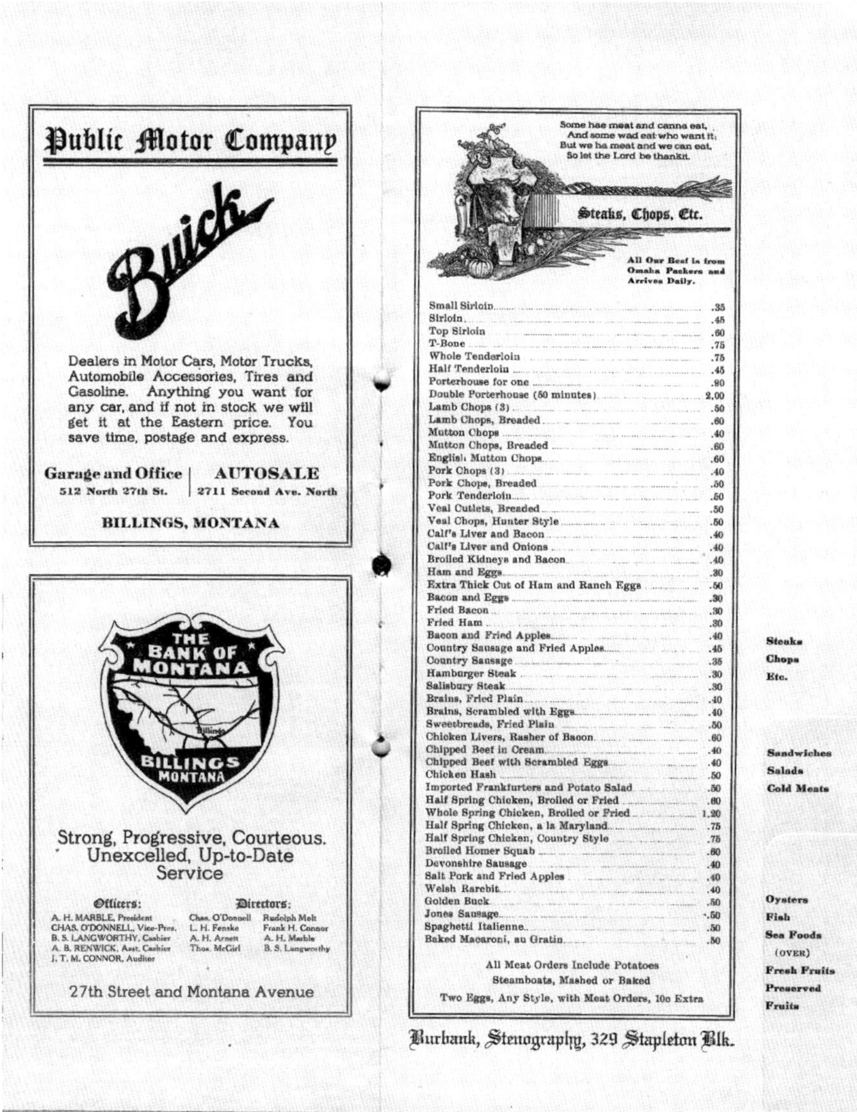

Public Motor Company

Buick

Dealers in Motor Cars, Motor Trucks, Automobile Accessories, Tires and Gasoline. Anything you want for any car, and if not in stock we will get it at the Eastern price. You save time, postage and express.

Garage and Office
512 North 27th St.

AUTOSALE
2711 Second Ave. North

BILLINGS, MONTANA

THE BANK OF MONTANA
BILLINGS MONTANA

Strong, Progressive, Courteous.
Unexcelled, Up-to-Date
Service

Officers:
A. H. MARBLE, President
CHAS. O'DONNELL, Vice-Pres.
B. S. LANGWORTHY, Cashier
A. B. RENWICK, Asst. Cashier
J. T. M. CONNOR, Auditor

Directors:
Chas. O'Donnell
L. H. Fenske
A. H. Arnett
Thos. McGirl
Rudolph Molt
Frank H. Connor
A. H. Marble
B. S. Langworthy

27th Street and Montana Avenue

Some hae meat and canna eat,
And some wad eat who want it;
But we ha meat and we can eat,
So let the Lord be thankit.

Steaks, Chops, Etc.

All Our Beef is from Omaha Packers and Arrives Daily.

Small Sirloin	.35
Sirloin	.45
Top Sirloin	.60
T-Bone	.75
Whole Tenderloin	.75
Half Tenderloin	.45
Porterhouse for one	.90
Double Porterhouse (50 minutes)	2.00
Lamb Chops (3)	.50
Lamb Chops, Breaded	.60
Mutton Chops	.40
Mutton Chops, Breaded	.60
English Mutton Chops	.60
Pork Chops (3)	.40
Pork Chops, Breaded	.50
Pork Tenderloin	.50
Veal Cutlets, Breaded	.50
Veal Chops, Hunter Style	.50
Calf's Liver and Bacon	.40
Calf's Liver and Onions	.40
Broiled Kidneys and Bacon	.40
Ham and Eggs	.30
Extra Thick Cut of Ham and Ranch Eggs	.50
Bacon and Eggs	.30
Fried Bacon	.30
Fried Ham	.30
Bacon and Fried Apples	.40
Country Sausage and Fried Apples	.45
Country Sausage	.35
Hamburger Steak	.30
Salisbury Steak	.30
Brains, Fried Plain	.40
Brains, Scrambled with Eggs	.40
Sweetbreads, Fried Plain	.50
Chicken Livers, Rasher of Bacon	.60
Chipped Beef in Cream	.40
Chipped Beef with Scrambled Eggs	.40
Chicken Hash	.50
Imported Frankfurters and Potato Salad	.50
Half Spring Chicken, Broiled or Fried	.60
Whole Spring Chicken, Broiled or Fried	1.20
Half Spring Chicken, a la Maryland	.75
Half Spring Chicken, Country Style	.75
Broiled Homer Squab	.60
Devonshire Sausage	.40
Salt Pork and Fried Apples	.40
Welsh Rarebit	.40
Golden Buck	.50
Jones Sausage	.50
Spaghetti Italienne	.50
Baked Macaroni, au Gratin	.50

All Meat Orders Include Potatoes
Steamboats, Mashed or Baked
Two Eggs, Any Style, with Meat Orders, 10c Extra

Burbank, Stenography, 329 Stapleton Blk.

Steaks
Chops
Etc.

Sandwiches
Salads
Cold Meats

Oysters
Fish
Sea Foods
(OVER)
Fresh Fruits
Preserved
Fruits

The morning menu from Luzon Cafe, 1943. *Courtesy of James M. Reich.*

In the spring of 1939, the Luzon closed for six weeks and was remodeled once again. On March 11 at 6:00 p.m., "Montana's Oldest Restaurant" showed off its new Vitrolite front, a "modernistic counter with matching stools," comfortable blond upholstered booths and "hand-finished walls of softest hue." This establishment continued to be open twenty-four hours and featured "those delicious steaks and dinners for which it is famous throughout America" at lowered prices, "as much as 40%." Even a year later, a "Plate Lunch" was offered at twenty-five cents.

A menu from the 1940s showed varied offerings that appeared to cater to many palates. Half a dozen "Oriental Dishes" from "Chicken Chow Mein" to "Chicken Chop Suey with Mushrooms" appeared on the menu. With breakfast served from 5:00 to 11:00 a.m., twenty-five cents bought a "Hamburger Steak, Potatoes, Wheat Cake or Toast with Coffee." The menu offered potatoes prepared in a dozen ways, including "French Fried, Hash Brown, Mashed, Lyonnaise, Cream Minced." To top the potatoes, "Fresh Salmon" or "Fresh Smelts" were "Gravies, Sauces, Etc.," which included "Country Gravy, June Peas, Tomato Sauce." "Canned Grapefruit," "Canned Peaches" and "Stewed Prunes" fell under the heading of "Fruits." Even oysters were offered when they were in season. A "Fountain Menu" included "Ice Cream Sodas—All Flavors," "Frappes," "Egg Drinks," "Refreshing Fancy Drinks" and even "Luzon Fruit Punch." Creamed, malted and phosphate refreshments and a category of "Ginger Ales" tempted customers into the café between main mealtimes. At the bottom of the menu was the ask: "If We Please You, Tell Others—If Not, Tell Us."

The Luzon Cafe was once again "Newly Redecorated" in 1948 and still serving "Excellent Food" with "Quick and Efficient Service." Frank Muster, who had been with the Mint Bar, took over the Luzon Cafe, with Rose Salamone as "chief chef" in 1951. The restaurant now served not only a "Complete Line of American Foods" but also "Italian Cooking." A year later, Rose and Frank's Luzon Cafe welcomed back Harry Pravis, a "Former Luzon Chef." At the time, the restaurant opened at 8:00 a.m. and closed at midnight, with a Saturday closing of 4:00 a.m.

The following appeared on the Luzon menu and encapsulated the spirit of the café: "All human history attests: That happiness for man—the hungry sinner—Since Eve ate apples, much depends on dinner." The Luzon Cafe may have been "the Leading and the Most Popular Cafe in Billings," with years of faithful service, but a claim it has definitely warranted is being one of Billings' oldest cafés.

5
THE STOCKMAN

"Where Men Meet Men"

The Stockman, located at 2805 Montana Avenue, was "Where Men Meet Men." This was the gathering place for real cowboys and those who wanted to be one. "Cowpokes, sheep-herders, stockmen, business executives, truck-drivers, railroad men, sportsmen, tourists…from all walks of life and from all vocations they come for relaxation and friendly chatter. Modern in every sense of the word, yet so unique in its old time western appointments and western hospitality that one should never miss a visit here while in Billings!" The Stockman was "Modern in Every Convenience," clinging to "Old-Time Western Traditions…Providing the Male Population of Billings and the Midland Empire with a Recreation Center Unlike Any Other in the Whole Northwest."

The place that provided this western hospitality was established in 1885 and claimed to be the "first class recreational center for men." In 1933, Quincy A. Edwards, Frank J. Rogers and J.B. Webster invested time and monies into further developing the enterprise. The institution provided its male patrons the "best in wines, liquors, and beers. The men upon whom the responsibility of serving the public rests pride themselves upon their ability to mix drinks and serve them well and courteously." Food was offered at the lunch counter. Also, a barbershop and recreational rooms were on site, and fishing and hunting supplies were available for sale, along with licenses for these activities. "All information in regard to sporting events is to be had, no matter where the event is scheduled. Complete reports are also given as soon as possible. Above all, you can meet your friends here for 'if he isn't in

Western Days in front of the Stockman Cafe, "The Reason I Forgot to Dress Western," 1940s. *Courtesy of the Western Heritage Center.*

the Stockman, he isn't in Billings.'" Edwards left the partnership toward the end of 1938.

The Stockman continued its western attitude and spirit in the 1937 *Billings Gazette* advertisement flashes entitled "hot shots…by the 'STOCKMAN.'" Each message began with the greeting, "Howdy Folks" from a fictional cowboy with a rugged, rustic and respectful sense of humor. Some thoughts included: "A man's word may be law in his own home, the wife is usually the supreme court." Another barb: "We've been told that our tobaccos please both the husband and wife. Here's a suggestion, men. Take her home a carton of her favorite brand and see how quickly you crawl out of the dog house."

In 1940, now under the ownership of Rogers, Webster and Les Fischbach, the Stockman became "The Midland Empire's Popular Meeting Place for Men" with "A Change of Menu Every Day." Of the food it was said, "To talk with a mouthful, but man oh man, I've never tasted such honest-to-goodness food. I thought it was too good to be true,

Inside the Stockman Cafe, circa 1940. *Courtesy of the Western Heritage Center.*

but long before I got down to the dessert and that delicious Electrobrew Coffee, I knew that the Stockman was the place to eat!"

Nine years later, in an advertisement entitled "Growing with Billings," the Stockman claimed to seat 39 people and serve approximately 2,200 people daily, with a staff of 92 and a payroll of $250,000. The offerings were "real man-sized meals," and hearty they must have been, for the Stockman tried to lure cattlemen to eat there when they were in town.

Drinks at the Stockman were served from a thirty-four-foot-long bar, with only the highest-quality liquor used in mixing the drinks. Of course, there was the promise that the customer would like the "Stag Bar," as it was the place for men who appreciated the "masculine comfort of a Sportsman's Retreat." Oil paintings by local western artist J.K. Ralson further provided the western ambiance, while the recreation room walls were decorated with thirty-six western murals capturing Leo Cremer's rodeo moments.

In the 1950s, Louis R. Hall joined the partnership. The Stockman advertised being open all the time and was prepared to cash checks. Hall recalled the day "the Stockman cashed more payroll checks than the banks in

A matchbook from the Stockman, "Where Men Meet Men." *Courtesy of Western Heritage Center.*

town put together." Hall remembered lines a half block long on paydays. By that time, the Stockman had 133 employees, including 3 barbers, and for years it held the record for selling the most fishing and hunting licenses in one season. Hall left the business in 1956.

The Stockman eventually closed at the end of July 1965. Addison Bragg reported stories of card games that went on for twenty-four hours a day, week in and week out, and of how more cattle was sold and bought at the Stockman than at the actual stockyards. Obviously, for eighty years, the Stockman was the place "Where Men Meet Men."

6

THE "CHOP SUEY" OF BILLINGS

CHINESE AND ASIAN RESTAURANTS

Ying Lee Custer's family came to Billings in 1937 when she was three years old. Her father, Chong Lee, brought his wife and five children from Loveland, Colorado, via Angel Island in the San Francisco Bay because he was to be a partner in opening the White Cafe. Unfortunately, he passed away a year after they arrived. With children to feed, her mother, Hom Lon York, took a job washing dishes at the St. Louis Cafe. Her two older brothers, David Fun Lee and Thomas Hom Lee, quit school and joined their mother at the St. Louis Cafe as cooks.

The St. Louis Cafe, serving both American and Chinese dishes, was located at 2507 Montana Avenue and was the longest-lived restaurant in Billings. The first evidence of its existence at this location, as listed in the *Polk City Directory*, was around 1912, with Charles Que as the proprietor and then Quong Lee taking ownership in 1916. However, according to the *Billings Herald*, the St. Louis restaurant existed much earlier and was purchased by L. Quock & Company on July 27, 1899.

In 1882, the year Billings was founded, Congress passed the Chinese Exclusion Act, which gave Chinese immigrants permanent alien status, barring them from becoming American citizens. Chinese workers arrived with the Northern Pacific Railway. These men took on some of the most dangerous jobs, such as boring tunnels and blasting mountainsides. At the same time, they organized themselves into a community on Minnesota Avenue south of the tracks.

In 1901, listed in the *Polk City Directory* for Billings were eleven establishments under the category of restaurants, five of which were Chinese names. Henry

The St. Louis Cafe menu cover, 1950s. *Courtesy of James M. Reich.*

Young, Lew Quock, Sam Young, Yee Ching and Yee Sam Lee owned restaurants located on Minnesota Avenue, while Sam Young operated on Twenty-seventh Street.

A police officer of the day remembered there were some ninety Chinese people in Billings who were mainly laundry and restaurant employees, born in China and with families still in their homeland. The Chinese lived close together, primarily at the east end of town near Minnesota Avenue. Sam Lee, one of the prominent Chinese businessmen, owned much of the block, including the L&L Building, which still stands at 2624 Minnesota Avenue.

The first names Lew, Leo, Lee, Lon or L. appeared in news bites with the last name Quock from 1899 to 1909 as a prominent businessman in Billings. L. Quock purchased the St. Louis Restaurant from Long Kong & Co. in the summer of 1899 and then renamed it the California Restaurant. The California Restaurant, located on the south side, offered "the best in the city," with "Regular Meals" for twenty-five cents. One can only imagine patrons finishing a meal and then stumbling over to Hannihan's Saloon next door.

Years later, in 1907, Leo Quock hosted eight prominent Billings businessmen to an eighteen-course feast made of rare and expensive ingredients. "Each and every dish was not only of Chinese preparation, but of ingredients strictly oriental in character and imported for the occasion." In the same year, the South Side Cafe opened. Though not listed under "Chinese Restaurants" in the *Polk City Directory*, this Chinese American restaurant was owned by Thomas Hee and located at 2604 Minnesota Avenue. Chinese Alley was found behind Hee's restaurant; here, opium,

South Side Cafe, 2604 Minnesota Avenue, 1907. *Courtesy of James M. Reich.*

cocaine and morphine dens provided a reprieve from the hard life on the Billings frontier.

Lee Quock also owned the Dr. Tuck Kam Medical Company, which sold Chinese medicines for curing many ailments. One could secure oils claiming to cure "neuralgia, rheumatism, stiff joints, headaches, colds, cough, stomach trouble and piles." The company also offered the "Celebrated Chinese tea" that remedied "biliousness, constipation and female troubles." In 1908, the company manager, Jack Fernandes, absconded with $750 of Quock's money. In an article written about the incident in the *Billings Gazette*, the tone was sympathetic toward Quock, reporting him as the proprietor of three restaurants and "several pieces of valuable real estate...By the business men he has always been considered as honest in his dealings with them, and a pretty square Chinaman."

By 1903, three Chinese restaurants—Hang Lem Kue, Quock & Quack and Sam Young—existed in Billings. Four years later, under the "Chinese Restaurant" heading, names such as Do Jack, Young You Chee and Toy Foy Sing appeared along with Quock's. A decade later, ten restaurants were listed under the category, while Japanese-named restaurants such as Tanihara & Kajikawa and Tomisaima Ichitaro appeared on the eating scene. At this time, Japanese workers were coming to Billings to work in the sugar beet fields.

In the early summer of 1938, proceeds in the amount of $246.75 from "bowl of rice" parties were sent to Colonel Theodore Roosevelt, the national chairman of the United Council for Civilian Relief in China.

CHOP SUEY

Pork Chop Suey.......... 55
Beef or Veal Chop Suey.......... 60
Chicken Chop Suey.......... 85
Green Pepper Chop Suey.......... 65
Lobster or Shrimp Chop Suey.......... 95

EGG FOO YOUNG

Egg Foo Young with Rice.......... 50
Chicken Egg Foo Young.......... 80
Lobster or Crab Egg Foo Young.......... 90

NOODLES

Plain Noodles without Meat.......... 30
Pork Noodles.......... 40
Pork Wor-mein.......... 55
Chicken Wor-mein.......... 80
Extra fine Chicken Noodles.......... 55

EXTRA SIDE DISHES

Chinese Broiled Pork, per dish.......... 35
Sesame Seed, per dish.......... 10

CHOW MEIN OR FRIED NOODLES

Pork Chow Mein.......... 60
Green Pepper Chow Mein.......... 70
Chicken Chow Mein.......... 90
St. Louis Specials.......... 60

CHOW FAN OR FRIED RICE

Pork Fried Rice.......... 45
Bacon or Ham Fried Rice.......... 50
Chicken Fried Rice.......... 75
Steak Rice.......... 50
Bowl of Rice.......... 15

PRICE FOR SMALL ORDERS OF ABOVE

Small Pork Chop Suey.......... 45
Small Beef or Veal Chop Suey.......... 50
Small Chicken Chop Suey.......... 70
Small Egg Foo Young with Rice.......... 40
Small Chicken Egg Foo Young with Rice.......... 70
Small Pork Noodles.......... 35
Small Chicken Noodles.......... 50
Small Pork Wor-mein.......... 45
Small Chicken Wor-mein.......... 70
Small St. Louis Special.......... 50
Small Pork Chow Mein.......... 50
Small Chicken Chow Mein.......... 80
Small Pork Fried Rice.......... 35
Small Bacon or Ham Fried Rice.......... 40
Small Chicken Fried Rice.......... 65

NO HALF PORTION SERVED ABOVE ORDERS

SINGLE ORDER SERVED TWO PERSONS 15c EXTRA

VEGETABLES

Radishes.......... 20
Green Onions.......... 20
Sliced Tomatoes.......... 20
Sliced Cucumber.......... 20
Celery.......... 25
Head Lettuce.......... 20

1

The back of the St. Louis Cafe menu with offerings of Oriental dishes, 1950s. *Courtesy of James M. Reich.*

Leon Shaw recruited several local restaurants—White Cafe, St. Louis Cafe, Commercial Cafe and the Palace Cafe—to serve bowl of rice dinners from 8:30 p.m. to midnight on June 17, 1938. At this time, Charlie Yee managed and owned the St. Louis Cafe with Sam Yee.

Because the St. Louis Cafe was open all day and night, the menu from the 1940s showed diversity. Breakfast was served from 5:00 to 11:00 a.m., with selections such as "Tomato or Orange Juice Toast and Coffee" for twenty cents and "Pork Chop Potatoes Wheat Cake or Toast Coffee" for thirty-five cents. "Waffles and Coffee," costing fifteen cents, were available all day. Categories such as "Potatoes, Oysters, Fish, Gravies, Sauces, Etc., Miscellaneous, Fruits, Drinks" offered options from hot to cold, raw to cooked, fresh to canned. Potatoes were "French Fried," "Lyonnaise," "Minced" or served as "Steamboats." Oysters came raw, in cream stew, fried or pepper roasted. Fish options ranged from fresh halibut to salted mackerel.

The "Miscellaneous" category proved further the efforts to please and to be enterprising and included "Chili Con Carne, 1 can," "Shredded Wheat Biscuits" and "Boston Cream Toast." Grapefruit and sliced orange were the only fresh selections in the "Fruits" heading, with the rest stewed or cooked

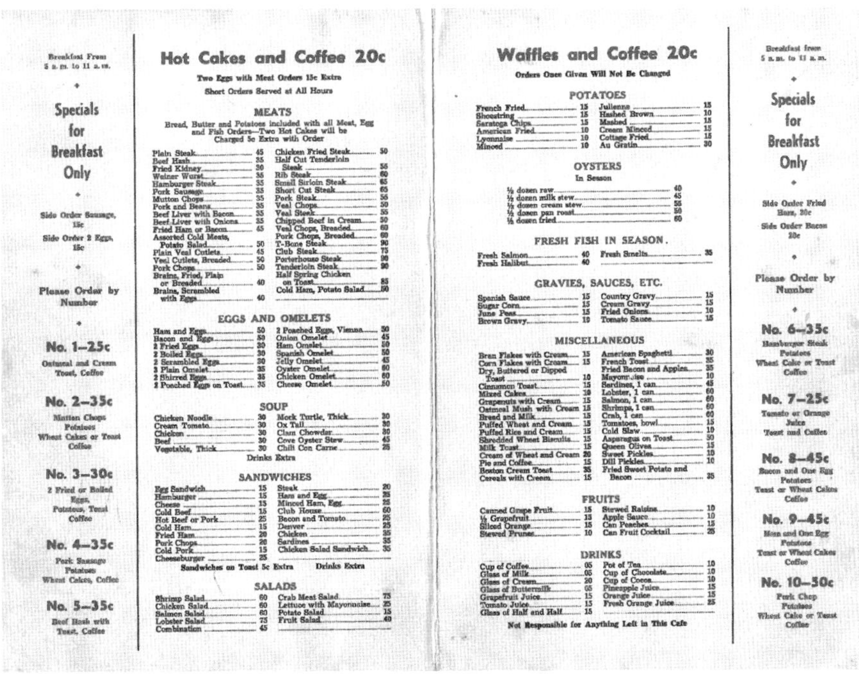

Breakfast From 5 a.m. to 11 a.m.

Specials for Breakfast Only

Side Order Sausage, 15c

Side Order 2 Eggs, 15c

Please Order by Number

No. 1—25c
Oatmeal and Cream Toast, Coffee

No. 2—35c
Mutton Chops Potatoes Wheat Cakes or Toast Coffee

No. 3—30c
2 Fried or Boiled Eggs, Potatoes, Toast Coffee

No. 4—35c
Pork Sausage Potatoes Wheat Cakes, Coffee

No. 5—35c
Beef Hash with Toast, Coffee

Hot Cakes and Coffee 20c

Two Eggs with Meat Orders 15c Extra

Short Orders Served at All Hours

MEATS

Bread, Butter and Potatoes included with all Meat, Egg and Fish Orders—Two Hot Cakes will be Charged 5c Extra with Order

Plain Steak	45	Chicken Fried Steak	50
Beef Hash	35	Half Cut Tenderloin Steak	55
Fried Kidney	30	Rib Steak	60
Weiner Wurst	35	Small Sirloin Steak	65
Hamburger Steak	35	Short Cut Steak	65
Pork Sausage	35	Pork Steak	55
Mutton Chops	35	Veal Chops	50
Pork and Beans	35	Veal Steak	55
Beef Liver with Bacon	35	Chipped Beef in Cream	50
Beef Liver with Onions	35	Veal Chops, Breaded	60
Fried Ham or Bacon	45	Pork Chops, Breaded	60
Assorted Cold Meats, Potato Salad	50	T-Bone Steak	90
Plain Veal Cutlets	45	Club Steak	75
Veal Cutlets, Breaded	50	Porterhouse Steak	90
Pork Chops	50	Tenderloin Steak	90
Brains, Fried, Plain or Breaded	40	Half Spring Chicken on Toast	85
Brains, Scrambled with Eggs	40	Cold Ham, Potato Salad	50

EGGS AND OMELETS

Ham and Eggs	50	2 Poached Eggs, Vienna	50
Bacon and Eggs	50	Onion Omelet	45
2 Fried Eggs	30	Ham Omelet	50
2 Boiled Eggs	30	Spanish Omelet	50
2 Scrambled Eggs	30	Jelly Omelet	45
3 Plain Omelet	35	Oyster Omelet	60
2 Shirred Eggs	35	Chicken Omelet	60
2 Poached Eggs on Toast	35	Cheese Omelet	50

SOUP

Chicken Noodle	30	Mock Turtle, Thick	30
Cream Tomato	30	Ox Tail	30
Chicken	30	Clam Chowder	30
Beef	30	Cove Oyster Stew	45
Vegetable, Thick	30	Chili Con Carne	25

Drinks Extra

SANDWICHES

Egg Sandwich	15	Steak	20
Hamburger	15	Ham and Egg	25
Cheese	15	Minced Ham, Egg	25
Cold Beef	15	Club House	60
Hot Beef or Pork	25	Bacon and Tomato	25
Cold Ham	15	Denver	25
Fried Ham	20	Chicken	35
Pork Chops	20	Sardines	35
Cold Pork	15	Chicken Salad Sandwich	35
Cheeseburger	25		

Sandwiches on Toast 5c Extra Drinks Extra

SALADS

Shrimp Salad	60	Crab Meat Salad	75
Chicken Salad	60	Lettuce with Mayonnaise	25
Salmon Salad	60	Potato Salad	15
Lobster Salad	75	Fruit Salad	40
Combination	45		

Waffles and Coffee 20c

Orders Once Given Will Not Be Changed

POTATOES

French Fried	15	Julienne	15
Shoestring	15	Hashed Brown	10
Saratoga Chips	15	Mashed	15
American Fried	10	Cream Minced	15
Lyonnaise	10	Cottage Fried	15
Minced	10	Au Gratin	30

OYSTERS

In Season

½ dozen raw	40
½ dozen milk stew	45
½ dozen cream stew	55
½ dozen pan roast	50
½ dozen fried	60

FRESH FISH IN SEASON.

Fresh Salmon	40	Fresh Smelts	35
Fresh Halibut	40		

GRAVIES, SAUCES, ETC.

Spanish Sauce	15	Country Gravy	15
Sugar Corn	15	Cream Gravy	15
June Peas	15	Fried Onions	10
Brown Gravy	10	Tomato Sauce	15

MISCELLANEOUS

Bran Flakes with Cream	15	American Spaghetti	30
Corn Flakes with Cream	15	French Toast	35
Dry, Buttered or Dipped Toast	10	Fried Bacon and Apples	35
		Mayonnaise	10
Cinnamon Toast	15	Sardines, 1 can	45
Mixed Cakes	10	Lobster, 1 can	60
Grapenuts with Cream	15	Salmon, 1 can	60
Oatmeal Mush with Cream	15	Shrimps, 1 can	60
Bread and Milk	15	Crab, 1 can	60
Puffed Wheat and Cream	15	Tomatoes, bowl	15
Puffed Rice and Cream	15	Cold Slaw	10
Shredded Wheat Biscuits	15	Asparagus on Toast	50
Milk Toast	15	Queen Olives	15
Cream of Wheat and Cream	20	Sweet Pickles	10
Pie and Coffee	15	Dill Pickles	10
Boston Cream Toast	35	Fried Sweet Potato and Bacon	35
Cereals with Cream	15		

FRUITS

Canned Grape Fruit	15	Stewed Raisins	10
½ Grapefruit	15	Apple Sauce	10
Sliced Orange	15	Can Peaches	15
Stewed Prunes	10	Can Fruit Cocktail	25

DRINKS

Cup of Coffee	05	Pot of Tea	10
Glass of Milk	05	Cup of Chocolate	10
Glass of Cream	20	Cup of Cocoa	10
Glass of Buttermilk	05	Pineapple Juice	15
Grapefruit Juice	15	Orange Juice	15
Tomato Juice	15	Fresh Orange Juice	25
Glass of Half and Half	15		

Not Responsible for Anything Left in This Cafe

Breakfast from 5 a.m. to 11 a.m.

Specials for Breakfast Only

Side Order Fried Ham, 20c

Side Order Bacon 20c

Please Order by Number

No. 6—35c
Hamburger Steak Potatoes Wheat Cake or Toast Coffee

No. 7—25c
Tomato or Orange Juice Toast and Coffee

No. 8—45c
Bacon and One Egg Potatoes Toast or Wheat Cakes Coffee

No. 9—45c
Ham and One Egg Potatoes Toast or Wheat Cakes Coffee

No. 10—30c
Pork Chop Potatoes Wheat Cake or Toast Coffee

The inside of the St. Louis Cafe menu, 1950s. *Courtesy of James M. Reich.*

New Moon Cafe. *Left to right:* Johnny Lee, Ying Lee Custer, Thomas Lee, Hom Lon York and Bill Lee. *Courtesy of Ying Lee Custer.*

fruits. Chow mein, chop suey and noodles made up the "Oriental Dishes" choices. The café then had a full "Fountain Menu" with sodas, sundaes, "Refreshing Fancy Drinks" with "Luzon Fruit Punch" and "Grape Juice Punch." Parfaits, frappes, cream and malted drinks, egg drinks, phosphates and plain drinks followed, with different brands of ginger ales finishing the refreshing treats available.

The St. Louis catered to a rough crowd, as firm statements appeared in bold print on the menu: "Orders Once Given Will Not Be Changed" and "Not Responsible for Anything Left in This Cafe." Because of the restaurant's hours and location, the St. Louis Cafe had its share of excitement. Reports exist of two Billings men fined twenty-five dollars for disturbing the peace after breaking the plate-glass window in 1912 and of Wyman Black being fined a ten-dollar charge of drunkenness in 1937. In addition, fights between Clyde Earl Clark and James Edward Kortje happened on occasion. In another incident, the café manager at the time, Wong (Slim) How, suffered "a blackened eye and the loss of several teeth."

In 1948, David and Thomas Lee started the New Moon Cafe at 4 South Twenty-seventh Street. This was a family affair, with their mother cooking breakfast. Ying Lee Custer, at age fourteen, remembered waiting tables at this intimate restaurant that catered to no more than twenty people at a time and featured an L-shaped counter and four booths for eating. Custer told of her brother David butchering all the meat. She said, "He could cook the best liver." His cooking skills took him to cooking at Gusicks Restaurant and the Northern Hotel.

Custer remembered a customer who worked at Chevron, Joe Malek, who came in for pancakes and would wait for her mother's short-rib sauce for his cakes. Even years later, Custer recalled the daily soup offerings: Monday—Alphabet, Tuesday—Seashell Macaroni, Wednesday—Barley, Thursday—Vegetable, Friday—Split Pea, Saturday—Anything and Sunday—Noodle. "They had steaks: plain steak, rib eye, sirloin and T-bone. They had halibut and shrimp." But Custer said the most popular dish was the "steak rice" with "small chunks of steak that was browned with onions and then thickened with water and soy sauce. The secret is to not overcook the meat."

Don Lee, David Lee's son, earned eight dollars for a whole day's work: "We had to put our money into savings. Both my brother and I learned the habit of saving. [After working for some time,] we had enough money to buy a house." The younger Lee did everything from washing dishes to waiting tables. "We worked on the weekends. Sometimes we would go to work at night…My father's pies were the best in the area—custard, apple, cherry, mincemeat pie. They sold out immediately. Then he made Jell-O desserts, stewed fruit." Lee continued, "Everything was made from scratch," including homemade noodles.

Wong Village was perhaps Billings' most iconic Chinese restaurant and was opened by Slim and Fay Wong in 1957. The restaurant offered "the very finest Chinese food, American food, Steaks-Seafood, Cocktail Lounge," with nightly entertainment from 11:00 p.m. to 3:30 a.m. The restaurant closed in 1995, but recipes have been preserved in the *Wong Village Cookbook* by its former owner Mitsuharu "Mitch" Hayashi, who began as a dishwasher and worked his way to partner in 1969 and finally to owner in 1985. He learned how to cook from Slim Wong, Tommy Hong and Richard Lee.

The restaurant was located in Lockwood, about one and a half miles east of the Magic City, and Karen Waddell remembered going there to celebrate birthdays as a child: "I always ordered the fried shrimp, but the best part was the Shirley Temple. In those days, a drink did not need a flower for it to be special." "It was the only exotic place to eat," Waddell recounted, recalling

Wong Village, "The very finest Chinese food, American food, Steaks-Seafood, Cocktail Lounge," closed in the late 1980s and is now a delicious memory. *Courtesy of the* Billings Gazette.

its popularity as a place for celebrations and special occasions. Ying Lee Custer's first date was at Wong Village, celebrating the Chinese New Year—Year of the Pig—with her now husband, Claude Custer, in 1971.

Susan Carlson, who attended Billings Senior High School, dined there with her prom date. An advertisement in the yearbook—"The right place to take your girl is WONG"—prompted teenagers to go there. Clint Peck recalled Wong Village as a small restaurant with low ceilings, ruby red crushed velvet and gold spray painted adornments. Peck said, "If you went to Wong Village, you were somebody. My parents thought it was expensive; it was exclusive." Peck remembered having the shrimp there too.

In recent history, C.W. and Lin Lin Lo opened the Great Wall Restaurant in 1987 at 1309 Grand Avenue. C.W. Lo, a fighter pilot for Taiwan Air, and Lin Lin, a piano instructor, relocated to the United States to provide educational opportunities for their two sons, Wayne and Ryan. In 2002, they retired briefly only to open Sweet Ginger two years later. The Asian-themed restaurant at 2515 Montana Avenue featured a sushi bar. At a quarter of the size of the Great Wall, the new eatery, designed by Mitch Thompson, featured dangling white rectangular lanterns in a room with royal Chinese colors of red, green and yellow. Large cloth prints of geishas and old family photographs graced the walls.

It is worth noting that Great Wall's neighbor Khanthaly's Restaurant, at 1301 Grand, owned by Khanthaly Keutia and her husband, Sisavath, served the first Laotian food starting in 1994 and for eight years. When their lease terminated, they offered their pad Thai noodles, egg rolls and fried rice out of a truck. Their mobile restaurant may have been one of the first food trucks in Billings. These days, they can be found at the Saturday Yellowstone Valley Farmers Market and during the week at the Transwestern II parking lot.

Jade Palace Chinese Cuisine held prominence off King Avenue in Billings' West End at 2021 Overland Avenue until the spring of 2015. Owners Stephen and Selina Tang retired after twenty-six years of running the Chinese restaurant that served Mandarin, Hunan, Szechuan and Cantonese dishes. The Tangs immigrated to the United States in the 1980s from Hong Kong, first moving to Cody, Wyoming, and finally to Billings to open the restaurant.

Marco Polo Gardens offered Mandarin-style Chinese food until 2002. The building at 1502 Grand Avenue was then torn down to make way for the second Montana location of the Missoula-based Mustard Seed Cafe, serving a pan-Asian brand of food. The Mustard Seed later became the Noodle Express Asian Bowls and was sold in 2013.

The Thai Orchid Restaurant, first opened in the mid-1980s at 20 North Twenty-seventh Street, was started by Thai native Lex Manraksa and Tony Chataransu. About ten years later, they relocated to 2926 Second Avenue North. Dorothy Sieler-Bonk and her husband, Kevin Bonk, bought half the restaurant in 1999 and purchased the entire establishment in 2001. A grocery store attached to the restaurant provided the first availability of Asian foodstuffs. The restaurant serving spring rolls and curries closed in 2004.

The building of the railroad introduced a cuisine from the other side of the world to Billings. The men who came here tried to reproduce their homeland's flavors utilizing the available ingredients. The result was inventive dishes such as chop suey (literally translated to "chopped pieces") and egg foo young. But mostly, the early restaurateurs learned to cook everything in an attempt to accommodate their customers. With their extensive menus, they demonstrated their ability to be flexible to service and satisfy the demands of varied palates. Later, as immigrants arrived from other parts of China and other Asian countries such as Laos and Thailand, the taste buds of those in Billings expanded and grew.

7

DRIVE-INS AND DINERS

Food and Fun

The spirit of the iconic films *Fast Times at Ridgemont High*, *American Graffiti* and *American Pie* stirred something in all of us. High school was a time-marked moment in our lives when we felt fast, fresh and free. The glossy pages of our yearbooks recorded the moments when we believed we owned the world and also provide a sampling of the diverse dining options in Billings. Diners, drive-ins and other eateries provided cool places to be. The Magic City had groovy hangouts that served burgers, shakes and pizza, as well as fancier fare, and for those who were not eating but just being a part of the scene, being seen was hip enough.

The Big Boy Drive Inn, Billings' first drive-in restaurant, tempted teenagers with its image of a boy holding up a double cheeseburger wearing a tank top and a low-waist diaper secured with a sizeable pin. He beckoned them with, "Hey Kids! It's Keen! It's Super!" The Slovak family started the restaurant at First Avenue South and Thirty-seventh Street in 1949. The Big Boy Drive Inn name was changed to the South Side Drive-in before Ailene and Tom Carr bought it in 1977 and named it King's Hat. The current owners are Vicki and Jim Hodgson. The restaurant located near the sugar refinery continues to bring in a good lunch crowd. According to cook Tyler Garrad, whose parents and grandparents owned the drive-in from 1977 to 2010, the most famous item is the flying burger. The burger is a fried hamburger patty between two slices of toasted, crustless white bread.

On the north side of the tracks, the Treat Drive Inn for "All Kinds of Ice Cream, Excellent Hamburgers, Chicken in the Basket" and Sandy's Thrift 'n

Swift Drive ("Open Year-Round") provided "Cleanliness-Service-Quality" as a treat for all, including families in the mid-1950s. Sandy's was where one could "Eat the Economical Way." In the 1960s, an ad in the *Billings Gazette* announced that a "3-Course Meal for a Family of Five" cost $2.25. "Pinch yourself when you get your bill at Sandy's Drive-in! Where else can you take your family and have everyone enjoy a pure all-beef hamburger, triple-thick, creamy [milk]shake and a bag of golden crisp French Fries for just 45¢." Ten years later, Sandy's had "2 Friendly Locations" at 511 Grand and 415 Twenty-fourth West and took on the snazzier name of Sandee's. The Sandy's chain was bought out by Hardee's in the 1970s.

For those who wanted to do some cruising, the Big Dipper Drive In located on Lockwood served up "cold pop, shakes, hamburgers, fries." In the mid-1960s, A&W Family Restaurant at the corner of Ninth and Grand Avenue opened its doors for customers coming "before the dance, after the game, or anytime in between. Home of the Burger Family." This was where "the Great Root Bear invites you on down to: 'Munch up our Menu. Where our food's as good as our Root Beer.'" On Friday nights, A&W ran a twenty-five-cent special for a fish sandwich with lettuce and tartar sauce.

Ice cream, shakes and malts offered delicious decadence. The Milky Way, located at 108 Poly Drive, had fountain and dairy service. Dorothy and Jack Rehberg owned the Milky Way for eighteen years and closed the operation in June 1970. "Hi-Quality Brand Dairy Products, Milk, Cream, Butter, Ice Cream, Ice Cream Novelties" were found at Billings Dairy. Burton's Candy Store brought even more satisfaction to the sweet tooth with "Delicious Candy" and fountain treats; so did Wilcoxson's Ice Cream and Candy Company. At Rimrock Mall, in the late 1970s to early '80s, Hipster-Doogan offered ice cream bars freshly dipped in chocolate and rolled in nuts and encouraged diners to "take a dip into the good life." Multi Flavor Ice Cream, with eighty flavors of ice cream and complete bakery and dairy compartments at 517 North Thirty-second, touted, "Our Ice Cream is Better than Good…It's Famous." In the late '70s, Baskin-Robbins Ice Cream Store came on the scene at 1212 Grand Avenue. Farther west, at 2150 Grand, Happy Joe's provided the balanced meal of pizza and ice cream.

This was the era when Coca-Cola advertised with such slogans as "Thirst, too, sees quality" and "Enjoy Yourself…Refresh with Coke." 7Up, NEHI with Royal Crown Cola and Pepsi-Cola were the other refreshments of choice. These thirst quenchers helped wash down Golden Spud Chips, "Tastee" pie and pastries from the Pie and Pastry Shop at 1145 Grand Avenue and Ideal Loaf Bread. Goodies Spud Chips were "Good Anytime or

Anywhere." For the graduate, the message from Goodies, with a caricature of a potato wearing a cap and holding a diploma, was: "No more teachers; No more books; No more sly flirtation looks; Nothing to do but smack my lips; All life long, on…" The chips were "crisp as autumn leaves. They taste delicious because they are always fresh."

For sit-down options, the *Kyote* 1955 yearbook for Senior High School held advertisements from the Coney Island Cafe for its homemade chili, the Sportsman Cafe for "Fine Foods, For the Whole Family" and the Stockman, "'Where Men Meet Men' Sports Headquarters for All Good Sportsman, Restaurant, Barber Shop, Sport Shop." Five years later, Tommy's Grill, Boe's Coffee Shops and the Turf Cafe enticed teenagers. Bob Porter, owner of the Turf Cafe, served up the all-American favorite hamburgers and French fries.

In 1965, the Butler Kitchens and Broasted Chicken Inn, owned by Mr. and Mrs. Howard Butler, advertised in the back of the *Kyote* annual with sit-in and drive-in options. For a family of four to eat in the dining room, twelve pieces of chicken; tossed salad and choice of dressing; hot rolls and honey; French fries and broasted potatoes; and coffee, tea, pop or milk cost $5.80. U.S. Choice and Top Sirloin Steaks started at $1.95, with "Bar B Que Ribs" at $1.75. Not only were prices comfortably affordable, but air conditioning provided for welcoming dining. The Billings West High School annual in the same year presented the Western Cafe at 1202 First Avenue North as the place for snacks or dinners.

In 1970, Sambo's Restaurant served "the nicest people with the greatest food," tempting the teenage set with "whipped-cream-topped strawberry waffles." Opened in 1957, Sambo's held prominence in the memory of many baby boomers. The chain that took on the theme from the children's book *The Story of Little Black Sambo* decorated its walls with images of a dark-skinned boy and tigers. Controversy over the promotional images and poor business decisions led to the closing of many of its restaurants.

The Windmill Club at 3921 First Avenue was "the place to eat after the formal" for "barbecue ribs, sizzling steaks, delicious shrimp and chicken in a basket." This dark and intimate supper club was a popular place for adults as well. The speakeasy peephole screened those who could enter during the darkest hours of the night.

In the 1979 *Broncs* annual, the image of a cute young woman behind the wheel of a Mustang convertible right next to a Yield sign captured the spirit of the times. The desire to be fast and wild was moderated with rules or with the want for the familiar. While hamburgers and fries remained ever so popular, pizzas and tacos emerged as delicious options. But there were also choices of old-fashioned homey food. Taco Johns, owned by Terry and Margaret Chirrick, said, "It's Tacorrific!!" and fed the masses with fast Mexican food. Later, Pork Chop Johns' "Butte Original Pork Chop Sandwich" became the "Great After the Game Treat!" At the Muzzle Loader Café, owner George Lundeen offered comfort food such as "Choice Steaks, Fried Chicken and Seafood Dinners" from 6:00 a.m. to midnight. To this day, the café makes a rib-sticking chicken-fried steak and rich biscuits with gravy.

From Mediocre Mike's (which made 5:00 p.m. to midnight pizza deliveries), to Guys and Dolls Casa de Pizza, "Makers of the World's Best Pizza," to Jail House Pizza and Beer and finally to the Shakey Pizza franchise, there were ample places to pick up a baked dough crust slathered with tomato sauce, cheese and other delectable adornments.

In exploring the West High School and Senior High School yearbooks from 1955 to the late 1970s, one can find a quick sampling of fresh, fast, exotic and new foods around town. By Chevy, Mustang or Trans Am—or even by foot—drive-ins, diners and parlors provided good food and a place to be seen.

8
WHERE'S THE MEAT

Steakhouses and Other Carnivorous Emporiums

To this day, a good thick steak can always be had in the city founded in 1882. The Rex, the Granary, Jake's and the Rib & Chop House are some of the iconic restaurants that have been known to satisfy appetites with quality slabs of meat. But cafés, diners and supper clubs, from the St. Louis Cafe, to Muzzle Loader, to the Elmo Club and the Windmill, offered generous bites of meat.

The most famous and historic steakhouse in Billings was, and still is today, the Rex, located on Montana Avenue. H. Alfred Heimer opened the Rex Hotel and the Rex Bar on March 27, 1909, with the help of his friend Buffalo Bill Cody. The sixteen-year-old German immigrant had taken a job with Buffalo Cody's Wild West Show in 1894. Though Colonel Cody fired Heimer three times the first day, the young man remained as a steward in Cody's private railway car until 1903. Heimer then settled in Billings to open his bar with brass foot railings, a metal ceiling and stained and beveled glass windows featuring a deep mahogany bar.

Acclaimed with the "Best Beer in Town," this was also where an authentic Dutch lunch and a glass of real Dutch beer could be found. The Rex Bar maintained that it was the "only place in the state having Imported Beer on draught brewed in Rotterdam, Holland." At the front corner of the bar was a deli where Heimer offered "Sausage and Meat Food Products of Highest Quality." The meats, secured from Weisel & Co. in Milwaukee, dangled in a glass case and included mortadella with pistachio nuts, New England ham sausage and Stuttgarter knackwurst.

The Rex in the 1970s, before the street closure. *Courtesy of the Western Heritage Center.*

The Rex Bar owned by H. Alfred Heimer, 1920s. *Courtesy of the Western Heritage Center.*

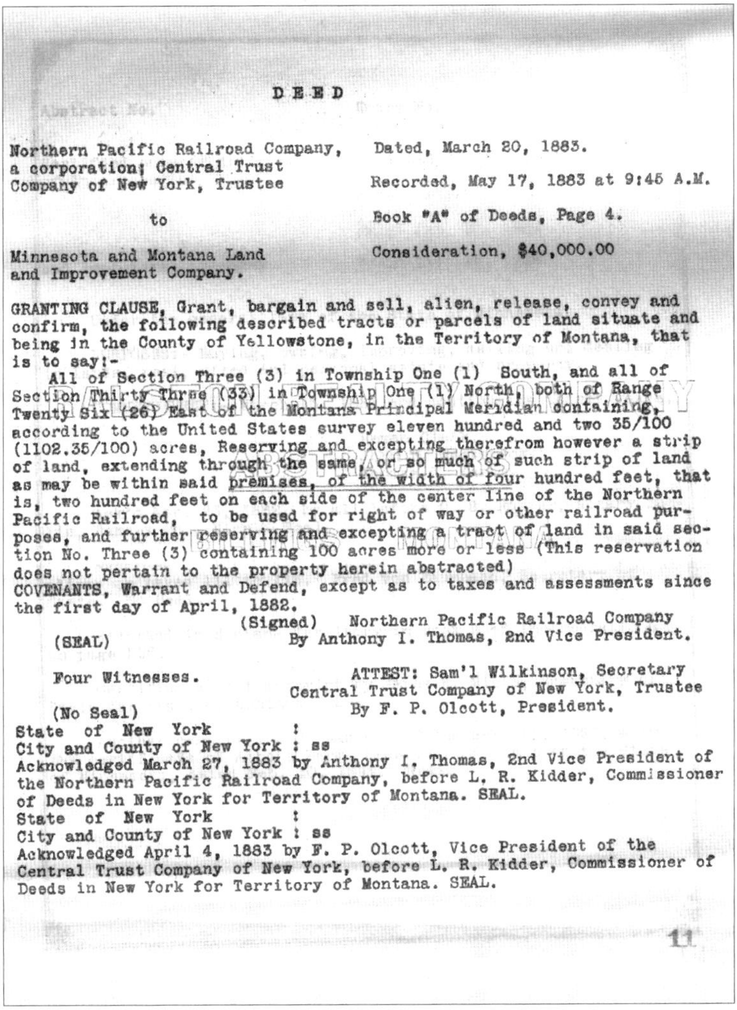

D E E D

Northern Pacific Railroad Company, a corporation; Central Trust Company of New York, Trustee

to

Minnesota and Montana Land and Improvement Company.

Dated, March 20, 1883.

Recorded, May 17, 1883 at 9:45 A.M.

Book "A" of Deeds, Page 4.

Consideration, $40,000.00

GRANTING CLAUSE, Grant, bargain and sell, alien, release, convey and confirm, the following described tracts or parcels of land situate and being in the County of Yellowstone, in the Territory of Montana, that is to say:-

All of Section Three (3) in Township One (1) South, and all of Section Thirty Three (33) in Township One (1) North, both of Range Twenty Six (26) East of the Montana Principal Meridian containing, according to the United States survey eleven hundred and two 35/100 (1102.35/100) acres, Reserving and excepting therefrom however a strip of land, extending through the same, or so much of such strip of land as may be within said premises, of the width of four hundred feet, that is, two hundred feet on each side of the center line of the Northern Pacific Railroad, to be used for right of way or other railroad purposes, and further reserving and excepting a tract of land in said section No. Three (3) containing 100 acres more or less (This reservation does not pertain to the property herein abstracted)

COVENANTS, Warrant and Defend, except as to taxes and assessments since the first day of April, 1882.

(Signed) Northern Pacific Railroad Company
By Anthony I. Thomas, 2nd Vice President.

(SEAL)

Four Witnesses.

ATTEST: Sam'l Wilkinson, Secretary
Central Trust Company of New York, Trustee
By F. P. Olcott, President.

(No Seal)

State of New York :
City and County of New York : ss
Acknowledged March 27, 1883 by Anthony I. Thomas, 2nd Vice President of the Northern Pacific Railroad Company, before L. R. Kidder, Commissioner of Deeds in New York for Territory of Montana. SEAL.

State of New York :
City and County of New York : ss
Acknowledged April 4, 1883 by F. P. Olcott, Vice President of the Central Trust Company of New York, before L. R. Kidder, Commissioner of Deeds in New York for Territory of Montana. SEAL.

11

Above: The deed for the property for the future Rex from the Northern Pacific Railway. *Courtesy of Gene Burgad.*

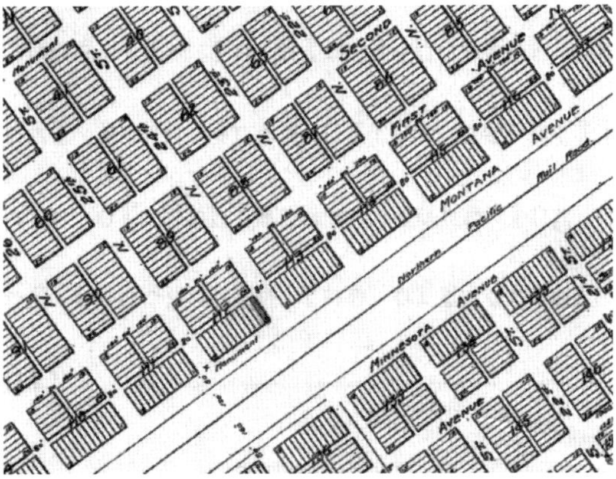

Right: The plat map for the Rex from 1909. This is a copy of the original plat from Lillis and Hatch Civil Engineers. *Courtesy of Gene Burgad.*

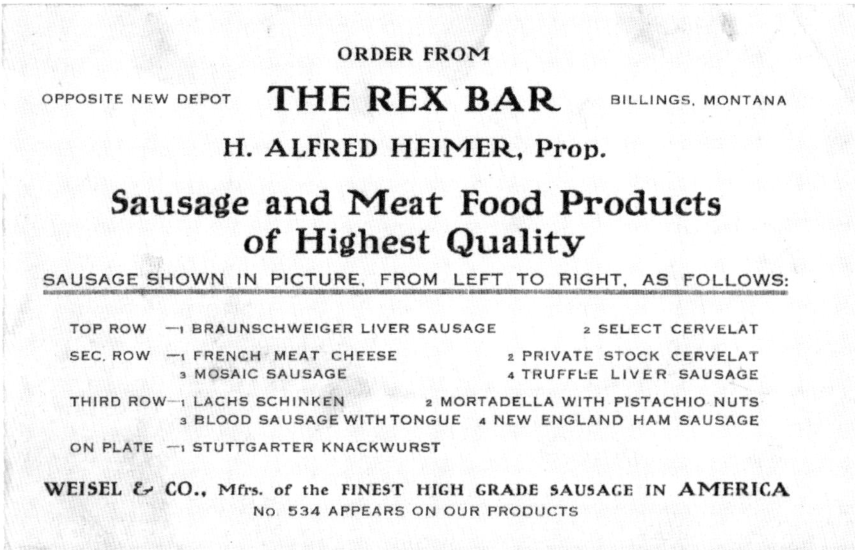

ORDER FROM

OPPOSITE NEW DEPOT **THE REX BAR** BILLINGS, MONTANA

H. ALFRED HEIMER, Prop.

Sausage and Meat Food Products of Highest Quality

SAUSAGE SHOWN IN PICTURE, FROM LEFT TO RIGHT, AS FOLLOWS:

TOP ROW —1 BRAUNSCHWEIGER LIVER SAUSAGE 2 SELECT CERVELAT

SEC. ROW —1 FRENCH MEAT CHEESE 2 PRIVATE STOCK CERVELAT 3 MOSAIC SAUSAGE 4 TRUFFLE LIVER SAUSAGE

THIRD ROW—1 LACHS SCHINKEN 2 MORTADELLA WITH PISTACHIO NUTS 3 BLOOD SAUSAGE WITH TONGUE 4 NEW ENGLAND HAM SAUSAGE

ON PLATE —1 STUTTGARTER KNACKWURST

WEISEL & CO., Mfrs. of the FINEST HIGH GRADE SAUSAGE IN **AMERICA**

No. 534 APPEARS ON OUR PRODUCTS

The back of a postcard listing meat and sausage offerings at the Rex curated from Weisel and Company. *Courtesy of James M. Reich.*

A postcard depicting meats and sausages offered by H. Alfred Heimer, proprietor of the Rex, 1920s. *Courtesy of James M. Reich.*

In 1917, a third-floor addition converted Heimer's hotel into one of the best places to stay at the time. "Important" citizens included the Crow chief Plenty Coups in 1921 as he was heading to Washington, D.C. More colorful celebrities included Will James and Calamity Jane.

During Prohibition, the bar moved from room to room. It was believed the Rex was connected to the underground tunnels that once existed in Billings, in which illegal alcohol was moved and delivered to customers. Gambling and prostitution may have become popular pastimes during this period, and it was purported these activities occupied the second and third floors of the hotel.

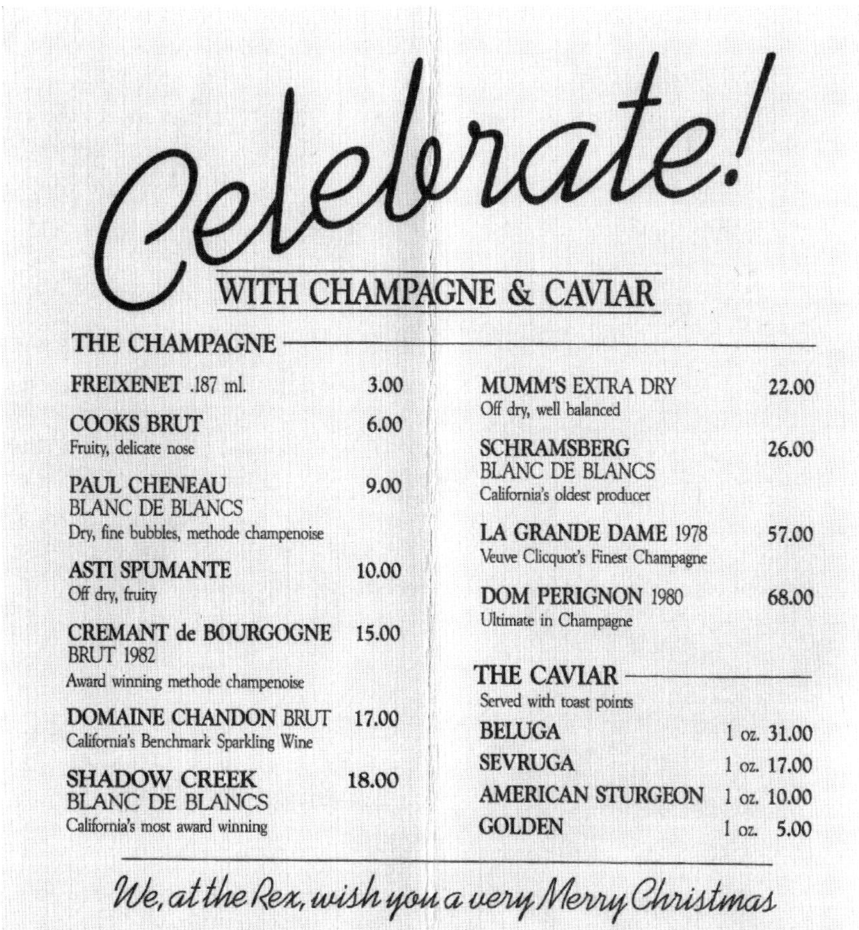

Celebrate!

WITH CHAMPAGNE & CAVIAR

THE CHAMPAGNE

FREIXENET .187 ml.	3.00
COOKS BRUT Fruity, delicate nose	6.00
PAUL CHENEAU BLANC DE BLANCS Dry, fine bubbles, methode champenoise	9.00
ASTI SPUMANTE Off dry, fruity	10.00
CREMANT de BOURGOGNE BRUT 1982 Award winning methode champenoise	15.00
DOMAINE CHANDON BRUT California's Benchmark Sparkling Wine	17.00
SHADOW CREEK BLANC DE BLANCS California's most award winning	18.00
MUMM'S EXTRA DRY Off dry, well balanced	22.00
SCHRAMSBERG BLANC DE BLANCS California's oldest producer	26.00
LA GRANDE DAME 1978 Veuve Clicquot's Finest Champagne	57.00
DOM PERIGNON 1980 Ultimate in Champagne	68.00

THE CAVIAR

Served with toast points

BELUGA	1 oz.	31.00
SEVRUGA	1 oz.	17.00
AMERICAN STURGEON	1 oz.	10.00
GOLDEN	1 oz.	5.00

We, at the Rex, wish you a very Merry Christmas

The 1986 Christmas champagne and caviar menu from the Rex. *Courtesy of Gene Burgad.*

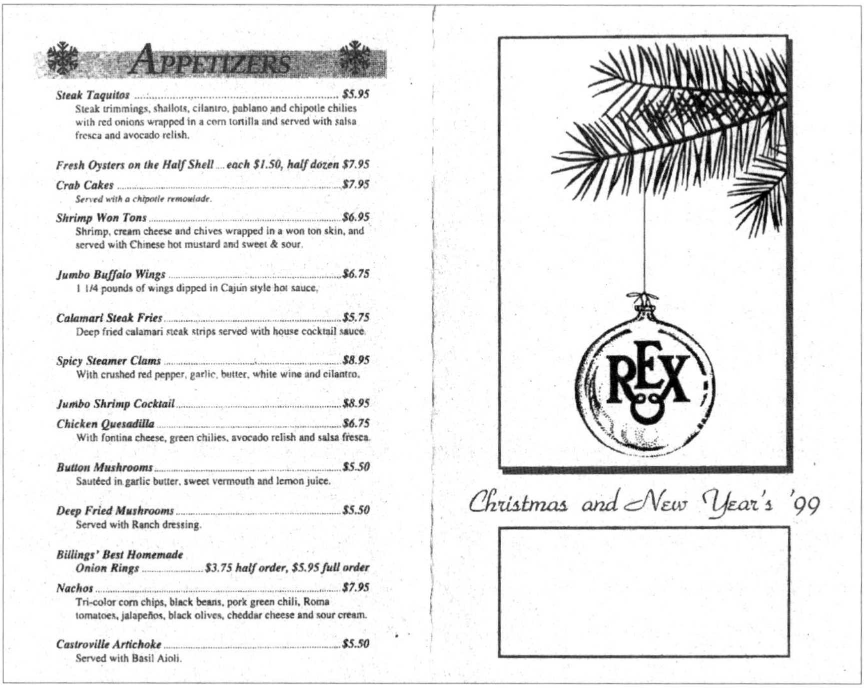

APPETIZERS

Steak Taquitos $5.95
Steak trimmings, shallots, cilantro, pablano and chipotle chilies with red onions wrapped in a corn tortilla and served with salsa fresca and avocado relish.

Fresh Oysters on the Half Shell ... *each $1.50, half dozen $7.95*

Crab Cakes $7.95
Served with a chipotle remoulade.

Shrimp Won Tons $6.95
Shrimp, cream cheese and chives wrapped in a won ton skin, and served with Chinese hot mustard and sweet & sour.

Jumbo Buffalo Wings $6.75
1 1/4 pounds of wings dipped in Cajun style hot sauce.

Calamari Steak Fries $5.75
Deep fried calamari steak strips served with house cocktail sauce.

Spicy Steamer Clams $8.95
With crushed red pepper, garlic, butter, white wine and cilantro.

Jumbo Shrimp Cocktail $8.95

Chicken Quesadilla $6.75
With fontina cheese, green chilies, avocado relish and salsa fresca.

Button Mushrooms $5.50
Sautéed in garlic butter, sweet vermouth and lemon juice.

Deep Fried Mushrooms $5.50
Served with Ranch dressing.

Billings' Best Homemade Onion Rings .... *$3.75 half order, $5.95 full order*

Nachos $7.95
Tri-color corn chips, black beans, pork green chili, Roma tomatoes, jalapeños, black olives, cheddar cheese and sour cream.

Castroville Artichoke $5.50
Served with Basil Aioli.

REX

Christmas and New Year's '99

The 1999 holiday bar menu from the Rex. *Courtesy of Gene Burgad.*

The Rex continued to prosper into the 1930s, '40s and '50s until the railroad business declined. The bar and restaurant continued to operate, with the upper floors falling to disrepair. The building was finally vacated and put up for sale. Then just one day before it was to be demolished in 1975, Senia Hart purchased the building. A year later, she sold it to A&E Architects, who brought life back to the building. The Rex Hotel Partnership purchased the business and building, remodeling the first floor to what it is today.

In 1990, Gene Burgad, one of the partners, expanded the restaurant into the adjacent North Twenty-fourth Street. Burgad shared that when he wanted to close off the street and build, "I had little hoops to jump through and make sure there was nothing underground. I had to go before the city council." He continued by joking, "Only the hospital and Gene Burgad can close off streets," relaying the challenges of his endeavor. The Rex was granted an Excellence in Historic Preservation Award by the Montana Preservation Alliance in 2006.

The Granary, located at 1500 Poly Drive, was erected in 1935. The building served as the milling department for Billings Polytechnic

Institute until World War II. Students from the institute (now Rocky Mountain College) produced flour and cereal. In 1976, it was reopened as a restaurant. Purchased by John Senner, John Peterson and Robert Vorachek, the Granary, a casual place that was "not as formal as the Rex," featured a salad bar, which offered "a dozen temptations for your lettuce ranging from sunflower seeds to diced onions and cherry tomatoes." "The one aggravation here is they don't accept reservations," and the wait could range from forty-five minutes to one hour during the dinner hour. A lounge downstairs provided live entertainment.

In 2004, Aaron Sparboe and John Scott took ownership of the restaurant. They hired John Beckner as general manager and Alan Sparboe, Aaron's brother, as executive chef. Extensive remodeling led to a loft and a dark wood bar with wood beams to retain the old mill feel. The addition of a wine cellar with a 2,500-bottle capacity offered guests an extensive wine selection. According to Sean McDaniel, before the renovation, a large tree shaded a wood-decked patio out back, creating a more natural and rustic ambiance.

On July 1, 2014, the Granary closed again for renovations after Jim Bos and his son, Kevin, purchased the restaurant. The new owners expanded

Jake's Steak House in the General Custer Hotel, built in the late 1800s. *Courtesy of Stella Fong*

the bar, decreased the size of the dining room and added a taproom offering twenty beers, mostly local and regional microbrews. In October, the Bos team reopened as Bistecca at the Granary, the Italian word for steak.

Jake's Bar and Grill opened in 1979 in downtown Billings in the old Hotel General Custer. The hotel was built originally as the Grand Hotel four years after Billings' founding. The hotel, before the turn of the century, was owned and operated by "Uncle" George Benninghoff and offered the first electric elevator and private baths in Billings. In 1951, three floors were added to the hotel, and on the seventy-fifth anniversary of the Custer massacre, the hotel's name was changed to Hotel General Custer. John Negu secured the best backdrop for his restaurant with metal ceilings and dark wood. Twenty years later, Negu, after traveling the Southwest visiting steakhouses, opened a 7,600-square-foot Jake's Bar and Grill on the West End at 2425 Gabel Road, where he utilized the architectural design talents of A&E Architects and the interior design of James Kordonowy of Homesite Designers to create a modern chic cowboy décor.

The Rib & Chop House was first opened in Livingston in 2001. It soon became a destination for many diners in Billings. Burke Moran, a former resident of Baton Rouge, Louisiana, and his wife, Melissa, brought the concept to Montana after success in Wyoming. Their motto, "Rocky Mountain Hospitality," continued when they opened in 2008, bringing their steaks and award-winning baby back ribs to Billings' West End.

Wander into establishments such as the St. Louis Cafe, Muzzle Loader, Elmo Club or the Windmill and a steak in all varieties, cooked to desired doneness, could be thrown on a plate accompanied with potatoes that were mashed, baked or fried.

One of the most mentioned and remembered meat palaces in Billings may have been Novasio's. This family-owned shop, known for its ten-cent "greasers," operated from 1929 into the 1980s at 17 North Twenty-ninth Street. It sold only burgers and fries. Randy Holbrook remembered going there and buying a brown bag full of sliders: "The bag shined with grease. They cooked them on a griddle with oil, half an inch deep." The ball of meat, dropped in a pool of grease and then flattened slightly with spatula, has lived in many memories from being on the scene for fifty years.

Though the Rex Restaurant Bar and Grill may have dominated the pages of history in Billings, a juicy steak or other meat could be found in almost any Magic City restaurant. The city the railroad created would not have it any other way.

9

JAMES HONAKER OF LA TOQUE AND BISTRO ENZO

Though short-lived, La Toque—founded in 1987 by James Honaker, Laurent Zirotti and Patricia Rolland—still lives deliciously in the memories of Billings' foodies. The modest restaurant served up cuisine in a French contemporary style decades ahead of its time. Then, for nearly ten years, the trio went their separate ways, only to reconvene and start Enzo Mediterranean Bistro.

La Toque—named after the French term for a tall crowned hat traditionally worn by chefs—showcased the culinary expertise of Zirotti and Honaker, who had cooked on both coasts of the United States and in Europe. In the thirty-six-seat establishment, the French contemporary cuisine challenged provincial palates. Fueled by youth and passion, La Toque sometimes only "did six or eight people," according to Honaker. Though they received laudatory compliments from those near and far who dined at the restaurant, their food did not resonate with most of the community.

Located at 123 North Twenty-sixth Street, the nondescript storefront, in a brick building with a plain panel of glass and a windowed front door topped with a round blue awning, led to a secret dining paradise. The intimate space, with white walls and white tablecloths, served "a daily menu fit for a French king." The sensual allure of La Toque continued with three life-size Freeman Butts paintings of nudes that graced one side of the dining room.

At La Toque, Honaker said of what he called "boutique French-style cuisine," "We were not worried if people would like the food." But Honaker admitted that "some dishes went over the top." He and Zirotti wanted to

La Toque, located at 123 North Twenty-sixth Street. *Courtesy of James Honaker.*

Wynton Marsalis with Laurent Zirotti and James Honaker on May 18, 1988, at La Toque. *Courtesy of James Honaker.*

James Honaker, Kurt Winegardner and Patricia Rolland in the kitchen of La Toque. *Courtesy of James Honaker.*

share the food they had learned to cook and loved. For about thirteen to twenty-three dollars, a diner experienced a four-course meal. Every day, a new menu was stuffed into a cover designed by artist Jon Lodge.

In an article written for the "Enjoy" section of the *Billings Gazette*, the then arts and travel editor, Christine Meyers, warned the diner, "Be prepared to treat your taste buds and your aesthetic sense because everything the three prepare is beautiful as well as delicious." Meyers's story described one of La Toque's appetizers: "A tartare of Oregon king salmon nearly guilds [*sic*] the lily, wrapped inside artfully smoked salmon."

After the salmon, Meyers told of the dinner proceeding to artichoke with local mushrooms, sturgeon with seasonal vegetables, roast duck with blackberries or rib eye with Roquefort sauce. La Toque was securing fresh fish and produce long before it was popular. Honaker said of the times, "People were just making the transition from steakhouse food. There was no Food Network."

Though these days his hair is gray at fifty-eight years young, Honaker still holds an uncertainty and shyness about the world around him. Currently, he single-handedly runs Bistro Enzo. As a chef, he finds harbor in the kitchen and shies away from public adoration. When obligation pulls him away from the galley, he hesitantly enters the dining room. In so many ways, this façade counters the deep passions and tenacity he holds within. His hard work earned him two nominations as a semifinalist for the James Beard Foundation's Best Chef in the Northwest in 2012 and 2013.

When talking to Honaker, his attention darts in many directions. It is almost impossible for him to sit still. His mind generates thoughts so quickly that he almost does not complete his sentences. After jumping up to answer the phone, he settles down long enough to talk of his cooking history only to bemoan wanting to update the décor of the dining room and then wanting to change his menu.

He tells of chapters in New York, his time in California and his annual pilgrimages to Formula One racing, though his roots are here in Montana. Honaker has always been torn between his affection for the Big Apple and the Big Sky. He first ventured to New York to pursue a career as a jazz drummer. During this period, he enrolled in cooking classes at Peter Kump's and then received his chef training at the New York Restaurant School. He subsequently cooked at the Windows of the World, where he gained wine knowledge from the wine director, Raymond Wellington.

Life then took Honaker to Napa, California, where he was a guest chef at Beringer's Winery and eventually cooked at Gerard's Brasserie in San Francisco. There he met Laurent Zirotti and Patricia Rolland. Then back to New York he went to attend film school on scholarship. Unfortunately, the award did not pay for all his expenses, so he needed to work. By good fortune, he ran into Chef Eric Ripert on the streets of New York City. Ripert's restaurant, Le Bernardin, had been open for two to three weeks, and since he was hiring, Honaker took on a cooking job.

Honaker vacationed with Zirotti at Flathead Lake, and there the idea of starting La Toque began. For two years, the Billings culinary rat pack of Zirotti, Honaker, Bill Elliott and Kurt Winegardner kept La Toque alive. Elliott helped with the front of house while Winegardner supplied the mostly French wine offerings. However, unable to meet financial margins, they had to close the restaurant.

Honaker returned to New York and worked at Le Boule and then apprenticed at Lenôtre to acquire bread-baking skills. Zirotti took on the deputy general manager position at the Hotel Majestic on the French Riviera in Cannes. In 1988, Honaker, Zirotti and the now Mrs. Zirotti, Patricia, opened Enzo Mediterranean Bistro on the edge of a Billings West End strip mall. The restaurant, with 140 seats under a terra cotta tiled roof in a farmhouse-style building, took on the name of the Zirottis' oldest son.

A takeout option named after their second son, Luca, never came to be. Both men shared the cooking, with Zirotti also taking on front-of-the-house responsibilities. With the Zirottis' movie star looks, customers were eager for the hugs and multiple-kiss greetings. Female diners, especially, looked forward to the charming welcome by Laurent.

The Zirottis struggled with immigration challenges during their time in the United States. Then the visions between the Zirottis and Honaker began to change. In 2008, after leaving Billings, the Zirottis opened their own restaurant, Fleur de Sel, in Post Falls, Idaho, serving country French fare.

Now the restaurant has taken on the name Bistro Enzo, and Honaker continues to serve American, French, Italian and Asian cuisine in a European ambiance.

10

MARIE HALONE

Changing the "Foodscape" with Level 3 Tea Room

In her Level 3 Tea Room in the Stapleton Building, Marie Halone served Billings the first slices of quiche Lorraine. From 1969 to 1983, she poured many spots of tea, served up countless bowls of Waldorf salad and dished up numerous portions of sour cream raisin pie. This petite, lighthearted woman with a steel core, who began her sentences with "Oh my goodness" or "oh my gosh" sprinkled with a few "oh Lordys," was the sugar and spice for all who entered her restaurant.

A few months before Halone's ninety-ninth birthday, we lunched in her home over strawberry and bleu cheese fresh greens salad and ham and broccoli quiche secured from Harper and Madison. Her good friends Norma Buchanan and Rhonda Molloy fluttered around her, attending to her needs, including setting up the table with her vintage pink dishware. Joanie Swords, proprietor of Harper and Madison and founder of the original Poet Street Market and, later, Dancing Oven Bakery, also joined us. Joanie's presence nostalgically reminded Marie of her times as the owner of the Level 3 Tea Room. An unsaid kinship—the joys and challenges of nurturing a place of celebration, gathering and nourishment—bonded these two women.

Marie worked hard. In her book, *Level 3 & Me*, she recounted, "It was such a busy kitchen in the mornings—so much to get done—and we were on that deadline every day, looking up at the big clock ticking away over the swinging door to the dining room." At first, Marie opened from 7:00 a.m. to 4:00 p.m., but she found that opening at 11:00 a.m. made life easier for her.

Rhonda Malloy, Marie Halone (ninety-eight years young), Joanie Swords and Norma Buchanan at Halone's home. *Courtesy of Stella Fong.*

Although "if a downtown businessman wandered by in the early mornings, we'd still serve them a scrambled egg and a cinnamon roll." She admitted, "I never stopped. I had to buy the groceries every morning. I had to go to the store by the tracks." Then she transported everything up in an elevator; she recalled how difficult it was when it stopped working on occasion.

Level 3 Tea Room began in the summer of 1969. Marie was taking an oil painting class when she overheard the other students talking about Senia Mabel Hart renovating the Stapleton Building downtown, with the goal of creating an arts and crafts gallery on level four with a tearoom below. Marie contacted Senia to express her interest in starting up the tearoom.

Although Marie had "zero" experience in the food business and even less handling finances, Senia's vision, great marketing skills and belief in Marie helped launch the business. Marie had cooked with her mother when she was a girl. "She did not do anything fancy. She did everything for everyday." Her mother made a cake her nephew Nathaniel (Daniel Anthony) named "buttermilk flat." Marie said her mother used buttermilk for everything, in the cake and in biscuits. When her mother offered to teach her how to make the cake, Marie declined because she believed if she made it, it would no longer be special.

In 1975, Marie attended La Varenne cooking school in Paris, France, which had just been started by Anne Willan and her husband, Mark Cherniavsky, for a three-week course in French cuisine. These skills she carried to the food in her restaurant, into the catering business and then to the cooking classes she taught in "the Barn." Marie bought the house in which she held her classes on her own, when her husband, Eugene, was out of town on a construction project. She had gone to the house after the owner passed away in hopes of buying wicker furniture she had seen on the porch, but in order to buy the furniture, she had to purchase the house. When Eugene returned home, he discovered he was the new owner of a house at 810 Poly Drive.

To get the tearoom ready in a matter of months, Marie enlisted the help of Eugene, recruited her mother for the sewing of napkins and other tasks and gathered friends who painted, sanded and pounded her space into shape. Her brother, Ralph Anthony, from the Cowboy Bar and Café in Meeteetse, Wyoming, taught Marie how to cook for large groups of people.

To this day, forty-four years later, Marie still remembers the column Addison Bragg wrote in the *Billings Gazette* on Wednesday, July 7, 1971. He mused about tearooms with no specific mention of Level 3 Tea Room, beginning with, "My masculine ego cringes at the thought of entering a tea room—even to drink a cup of tea." But it was obvious Marie took his humorous steroid-studded comments to heart. She still remembered Bragg's last sentence: "I'm just saying that the guy who needs a hamburger, rare, with a slice of raw onion, toast the bun and hold the mustard and chips, can get in a tearoom—but probably by the time it comes he'll wish he hadn't."

Marie said of Bragg writing about her place, "It was nice but in a bad way." When he came into the tearoom after that column, Marie threatened, "I am going to sue you." As he turned white, Halone added, "You did not write a nice thing about my tearoom." Bragg's defensive response was, "I wrote it in a different kind of way so a man could read it." With a wry smile, Marie continued, "I just wanted to scare him, and he was for a minute or two."

But in 1979, the *Billings Gazette*'s "Dining Out" section indicated that Marie had changed her menu to accommodate demand. She was quoted as saying, "We sell so many hamburgers that sometimes we feel like Ronald McDonald's big sister. But they're so good—quarter pounders made of the best beef—that if we took them off the menu we'd have puddles of tears all over the place."

Level 3 Tea Room provided for many gatherings—birthday parties, bridge luncheons, showers and so much more. Lynda Moss, when she came to Billings in 1981 as the curator of education at the Western Heritage

Center, shared, "Level 3 Tea Room was my first introduction to the culinary collection in Billings." The large shared table in the restaurant introduced her to many people in the community. At one time, a restaurant in Billings offered "Sherried Mandarin Orange Mold" with finger sandwiches and "Sea Foam Meringue with Raspberry Chantilly Filling." Marie admitted in her book, "I never dreamed in the 11 years at the tea room that we were part of the history of Billings. I learned later how much of an influence we had on the local 'foodscape,' causing people in the community to be more adventuresome with what they cooked and ate."

11

CARL KUROKAWA

A Loud Passion for Food

Carl Kurokawa, executive chef and proprietor of Juliano's Restaurant, has been cooking in Billings for over twenty years. In March 1995, he purchased the forty-seat establishment at the edge of downtown in the hospital corridor with Dave McCurdy and Tim Keating. In the stable building that serviced the neighboring 1902-built Austin North House, more popularly known as "the Castle," Kurokawa created his own delicious history. Many a toast has been made in the multi–dining room space.

With a Fu Manchu mustache and six-foot stature, Kurokawa exudes confidence. His baritone voice booms self-assurance, amplifying his irreverent personality. His ability to speak his mind provides an honesty that actually endears people to him. Kurokawa knows everyone, and everyone knows him.

It was that relationship with people that brought him to Billings, Montana. Kurokawa crossed paths with Kurt Johnson and Dave Creekmore when they were visiting Hawaii. In the mid-'70s, Kurokawa came to Big Sky country for the first time as a tourist, which set the attraction and attention for him to this part of the world.

After completing the culinary program at the Hawaii Community College in Hilo, he worked for a couple years in the industry. Feeling as though he had gone as far as he could working at hotels and resorts in Hawaii, such as the Kona Surf Hotel and apprenticing at the Mauna Kea Beach Hotel, he came to Montana. "Bottom line is after my apprenticeship I felt good enough to work anywhere in the world. I could figure it out, and I did not even have

Above: Juliano's Restaurant, where Carl Kurokawa was executive chef for over twenty years. *Courtesy of Stella Fong.*

Left: Juliano's Restaurant was a 1902 converted stable with patio as a backdrop for inventive Asian-accented American cuisine. *Courtesy of Stella Fong.*

to know the language." Kurokawa tells of arriving on the mainland, "I came over here with a couple of suitcases and a box of books."

Before cooking with Paul DeVerniero at DeVerniero's Ristorante, Kurokawa was at the Riverside Country Club in Bozeman and the Twin

Lakes Village in Coeur d'Alene. He confessed, "Just my brashness got me the jobs." He spent a year at the Northern Hotel and then moved on to the Sheraton, where he married his "salad girl."

"My wife is very supportive. We met in the business, so she understands. We have been married for thirty-three years. My cooking instructor once told me, 'You have a wife and you have a mistress. Your restaurant is your mistress.'" Kurokawa's obsession with work is further evidenced by his admitting, "I don't have a cellphone because I don't need one. I am here or I am home."

These days, Kurokawa serves no more than forty covers a night, as he believes this is the maximum number he can comfortably offer for ultimate food quality and service. Kurokawa has a staff of eight people, with half working the front of the house and the other half in the kitchen. His core staff has been with him since he opened. Even the heart of his menu has remained the same. Kurokawa would not dare remove his "Crispy Battered Chicken and Grapefruit Salad" with citrus vinaigrette and honey-roasted pecans. His customers would revolt if he took away the "Warm Flourless Chocolate Cake" with Chantilly cream and chocolate sauce, garnished with Kurokawa's signature of fine wispy sugar strands.

Kurokawa describes his food as "fun American with European and Asian influences." Dishes such as "Kona Coffee Crusted Rock Mountain Elk Medallion" and "Caramelized Pineapple Glazed Duckling" with tart and sweet pineapple and pepper sauce and scallion fried rice summarize his style. He is playful with his offerings and will present dishes such as "Hot Dog and Fontina Cheese Melt" wrapped in smoked bacon with tomato-jalapeño relish and "Almond-Encrusted Frog Legs" over fresh Thai salad and sambal aioli.

The name "Carl's Restaurant" would have been more fitting for Kurokawa, but his partners wanted to keep the original name that had been established two owners back. According to Kurokawa, the name came to be by combining the first name Julie with her middle name, Ann. Coincidentally, Carl's wife's name is also Julie. Actually, Kurokawa wanted to name the restaurant "Yasu" after his father and his son's middle name. "Twenty years ago, restaurants had names like Spagos and Nobu." In Japanese, *yasu* means peaceful and tranquil. With a smile, Kurokawa continued, "In Greek, it is a greeting," something that comes naturally to Kurokawa with his personality and food.

Kurokawa was serving "local" food long before it was popular. "Last fall, I went over to Charlie Yegen and told him I wanted to buy a steer. He says okay. Then a couple of months later he calls me up. He comes down for lunch, and then I meet him at the corral and I tell him the number of the cow I like. We load him up on the truck and we take him to the feedlot. We put him on feed ninety days. I get back from Hawaii and I pick up the packages from Stillwater Packing."

In the fall, he purchases lamb raised by Annabel Lombard in Fromberg, and for years he has had a Northwest wine list. In 2003, Kurokawa continued his support of Montana products when he was sent to Japan by the Department of Agriculture. There, he prepared dishes with Angus beef, Grains of Montana flour and paddlefish caviar from Glendive.

He continues to support the Montana Chefs and Cooks Association that he helped establish. He still supports the annual Montana State University–Billings Wine and Food Festival after teaching one of the first cooking classes with Alexander Valley Vineyards. He has cooked for Kent Rosenblum of Rosenblum Cellars and Ed Sbragia of Beringer Vineyards. To this day, Kurokawa loves doing special parties and still continues to have his annual cigar and lamb dinners. "I love the connection with the people who come here. I encourage them to have a good time."

If the Bacchanalian images on the tin ceiling of one of his dining rooms could talk, we would hear words of celebration and cheer and so much more. Though Kurokawa may dream of retiring and becoming a dishwasher in an old funky restaurant somewhere, for now, he will continue to share his loud passion for food and people.

12
WALKERS

Bill Honaker, Mike Callahan and Randy Holbrook

To step from the cold street and into the foyer, and then to slip down the stairs to Walkers Grill, a diner felt special. Sophistication and simple elegance emanated from the Craftsman-style room, and the sense of being announced when stepping down into the main dining room extolled grandeur.

In 1993, brothers Bill and James Honaker opened Walkers Grill in the basement of the historic chamber of commerce building downtown, changing the food scene. The restaurant quickly became popular and even attracted President Bill Clinton to dine there in 1995.

Bill Honaker had helped his brother James when he operated La Toque with Laurent Zirotti back in 1987. He washed dishes and did the books. Then he went to Philadelphia to pursue work in real estate and ended up working part time at Jack's Firehouse. "I went into Jack McDavid's Firehouse and asked him if I could work for free. I had to go back three times," Honaker said. There, he met Mike Callahan, who was the sous chef and became Honaker's boss. At the Firehouse, Honaker learned about the workings of the kitchen and the philosophy of farm to table.

When Honaker returned to Billings and decided to open a restaurant, he called Callahan. Naming the restaurant after his late father and recruiting his brother James to help made this a family affair. Callahan arrived in Montana in January 1993. "We worked on the restaurant for a couple of months and opened it in March or April," Callahan relayed.

In the space before Walkers was Cellar 301, a breakfast and lunch restaurant. Jeanne Moller, who waitressed there, remembered people coming

Walkers Grill in the basement of the historic chamber of commerce building, 1993. *Courtesy of Bill Honaker.*

in just to see the décor. The establishment, in a shade of green with loud floral wallpaper and black-and-white tile, was quickly refurbished with the help of Mitch Thompson. Jazz music replaced the live piano tunes played at lunch, and the famous Cellar baked beans was replaced with handmade pasta and locally sourced fare and the meatloaf that became an iconic dish for Walkers. Finally, Frank Lloyd Wright would have been happy with the completed interior design.

Randy Holbrook, who had just returned to Billings from the Twin Cities, was the first official employee at Walkers. He had solicited the other restaurants in town and one day cold called Walkers before it was even considering hiring workers. When Holbrook arrived at the restaurant, James had to dig out an application. When the "huge cattle call came," as Holbrook described the process, hundreds of applicants submitted their résumés. Holbrook believed his confession of not having much knowledge of food got him the job. "Jim and Mike knew that you never know enough about food. You are always learning." Holbrook ended up waiting tables, prepping, cooking on the line and establishing the wine menu.

"We were extremely successful right off the bat. It was extremely strong for the first three to five years," Callahan confessed. "It was my favorite restaurant to work in because there were no boundaries. We were a combination of everything," Callahan shared. Honaker distinguished his food as "New American Cooking," inspired by Alice Waters of Chez Panisse in Berkeley, California.

Callahan described the experience with President Clinton's secret service as interesting. He remembered insisting on taking the coat of one of the agents. "They have to wear full gear, and this guy was sweating because it was so hot." After further insistence, the agent revealed to Callahan all the guns he was carrying on his body to protect the leader of our free world. "We had a choice of two entrees, but he [Clinton] ate both, venison and salmon." After dinner, Clinton came down from the upstairs dining room into the kitchen and shook hands with the staff. To this day, there is a photograph of Clinton and the Walkers staff recording this memorable day.

In 1998, James left Walkers and opened his own restaurant in the West End, Bistro Enzo. Then, in 2003, Bill moved across the street from the Sheraton Hotel, now the Crown Plaza, to 2700 First Avenue North. The new street-level Walkers American Bar and Grill and Tapas Bar took on the feel of city cosmopolitan tempered with cowboy chic. A hand-forged floor-to-ceiling two-hundred-bottle rack created by Craig Whiteley behind the long wood bar

DINING & ENTERTAINMENT

DINING & ENTERTAINMENT

WALKERS GRILL

"Unsurpassed in this area... Walkers rewards with every bite!"

Christene Meyers, Arts and Travel Editor, The Billings Gazette

Small Plates, Soups & Salads	**$3-$7**
Mediterranean Pizzas & Pastas	**$5-$10**
Steaks, Chops, Birds & Fishes	**$9-$17**

Featuring exclusive dry aged Montana beef!

"Casual City Dining in the Historic Chamber Building"
301 North 27th Street — Only 2 blocks from the Billings Sheraton Hotel
Bar opens at 4:00 pm — Dining Room at 5:30 pm
Reservations accepted • Phone 245-9291

A-7

The menu from Walkers Grill, "Casual City Dining in the Historic Chamber Building." *Courtesy of Bill Honaker.*

dominated and showcased the cocktail lounge. Suede, leather and horse reins, along with light fixtures of twisted barbed wire, contributed to the sense of the West. Gordon McConnell's murals of cowboys in the dining room croon the romance of a cowboy's life.

Over the years, Honaker's customers have included Bruce Dern and his daughter Laura, Jon Voight and Angelina Jolie and many other celebrities. But the guests he feels the most sentiment for is the couple from Wyoming who were the first ones to be engaged at the restaurant. This couple returns every year to celebrate their anniversary. Honaker said his count is eighty-seven for the number of engagements occurring at Walkers. Finally, he told of his most famous local guest: "Mrs. Fortin used to come in all the time. She wanted an armed chair and a round table that would fit fourteen to sixteen people." Mary Alice Fortin is honored along with her husband, Phillip, with the Mary Alice Fortin Health Conference Center at Billings Clinic, the Fortin Lobby at St. Vincent Healthcare and the Fortin Education Center at Rocky Mountain College.

After over twenty years in the restaurant business, Bill Honaker wanted to share: "My philosophy is making people happy, if you can do it in life. If people are better internally, then it is the biggest thing I am proud of." Even more, the spirit of Walker Honaker should be most proud of how many people his son has made happy.

13

MIKE SCHAER'S MONTANA AVENUE

Creating a Taste of the Old Chicago Neighborhood

For over thirty years, Mike Schaer has re-created a taste of his childhood neighborhood on Montana Avenue. "I came from Chicago, and we lived on the extreme south side off of Michigan Avenue." Fondly, he remembered the street enlivened with theaters, restaurants and stores. These days, Montana Avenue, the artery running west to east found just north of the railroad tracks downtown, anchors more than a dozen businesses—restaurants, two breweries, a distillery, several art galleries, a performing arts center and the restored train depot.

At one point in the early 2000s, Schaer laid claim through leases and ownership to a Mexican restaurant (Don Luis), an Asian eatery (Sweet Ginger), a bakery and café (Log Cabin), an upscale restaurant (Q Cuisine), a nightclub and martini bar (Club Carlin), an Italian eatery (Cafe Italia) and a lunch and coffee house (McCormick Café).

Schaer recalled growing up in a safe neighborhood where he, as a child, freely navigated and explored. He helped his cousin deliver newspapers from 103rd to 115th Streets. "I had one side and he had the other side. We went to school with just a couple of kids. I do not remember my mother ever taking me."

When Schaer relocated his company, Computers Unlimited, to Montana Avenue in 1983, he knew he needed to change the landscape and culture. He bought three buildings—2405, 2407 and 2409—to refurbish for his operation. At that time, prostitutes and derelicts frequented the area, with pigeons taking over unoccupied buildings. Over three decades, he purchased

Log Cabin Tavern, U.S. Cafe, St. Louis Cafe, Hotel Carlin and Billings Brewing Company on Montana Avenue, 1940s. *Courtesy of James M. Reich.*

properties on the avenue, releasing buildings by selling to buyers with the same reenergizing vision he possessed.

In 2003, Schaer sold the Marshall-Wells Building (more recently called the Grinnell Building) to CTA Architects for $400,000, the price he had paid for the building, to help facilitate development. Then he convinced Venture Theater to move from its small space on Central Avenue to Montana Avenue. He does not recall the exact conversations, "but I think the low cost for the facility and extremely low payments and low, low interest" sealed the deal.

In 1994, Vicki Van Buskirk, owner of the Toucan Gallery, and Judy McNally, president of the Billings Preservation Society, teamed up with Schaer to remove abandoned vehicles from the street and install streetlights in the alleys. A half dozen years later, a streetscape project continued improvement with the installation of decorative planters, ironwork and lighting. The work done corresponded to Schaer's theory in preventing the transient problem: "Light it, pave it and do not provide a place to sit down."

That same year, Gene Burgad bought and remodeled the Rex, while Schaer bought more neighboring buildings. Today, the Rex Restaurant Bar and Grill has become the iconic steak restaurant specializing in certified Angus beef and fresh seafood. When Schaer bought the McCormick Hotel building, originally built by farmer William H.

McCormick in 1905, his initial intention was to turn it into an Internet café. But "I came to the conclusion that Internet cafés do not work here in Billings because people have computers at home. Then I converted it to a restaurant." The McCormick Café, retaining the brickwork and tin ceilings, opened for business on May 1, 1998, and to this day serves only breakfast and lunch. It is touted as a place "Where Locals Eat!"

Abby Hinthorne helped Schaer start the café. Having been raised in a Hutterite colony, Hinthorne learned at a young age to cook for a large crowd. Many of the dishes she created took on names of local businesses. The offerings, written in colorful chalk lettering on a large blackboard, provided for easy ordering at the counter. Hinthorne continued on into the food business by opening her own company with her husband, Tom, Abby's Catering.

In the summers, Schaer sported an apron as he teamed up with his wife, Cara, to make and sell crepes offered on the McCormick Café menu to customers of the Saturday morning Yellowstone Valley Farmers Market. After he cooked the crepes, she dressed them with chocolate hazelnut butter, lemon juice and powdered sugar or raspberry coulis. A line forming in front of their booth before the ringing of the Farmers Market start bell was a regular weekly sight.

Q Cuisine and Club Carlin, located at 2501 Montana Avenue, were the cornerstone restaurants and bar in Schaer's neighborhood. In 2002, he remodeled the 1910 Hotel Carlin that once catered to railroad passengers. While Club Carlin Martini Bar and Nightclub and Q Cuisine Restaurant anchored the lower level, the upper level offered one of Billings' first extended-stay suites as respite for tourists and business travelers. For a short while, Schaer showed foreign films one night during the week in the Club Carlin space.

Q Cuisine served traditional American bistro food infused with contemporary and cosmopolitan fare. The space, reinvented with the help of designers Mitch and Melanie Thompson, transported the diner from Montana Avenue to places afar. Romance, sophistication and whimsy exuded under the original stamped tin ceilings in a space filled with fanciful colors and rustic materials. It would have been no wonder if Alice had walked through one of the wall mirrors from Wonderland.

Schaer convinced his daughter, Suzy, to return to Billings to help him start the restaurant and bar. At the time, in 2000, Suzy lived in Los Angeles and worked for Sheraton Universal Hotel in the marketing and management department located in the back lot of Universal Studios. Because Suzy's coastal friends called her "Q" and "Das Q," Schaer's new enterprise took on the name of Q Cuisine.

With Suzy came her soon-to-be husband, Daniel Roberts, who had just completed studies at Le Cordon Bleu College of Culinary Arts in Los Angeles. For almost a decade, Daniel took on the executive chef position while Suzy ran the front of the house. Their success culminated with Daniel's 2011 nomination as a semifinalist for the James Beard Foundation Best Chef in the Northwest Award. But with the challenges of operating a bar and a growing family, the restaurant closed a few years later.

In the next years, Schaer sold the Yellowstone Garage—which had housed an artist co-op, Rue des Artistes—to brothers Matt and Jake Brosovich, who in 2009 opened Ciao Mambo, a chain headquartered in Whitefish, Montana. The space next door became home to Überbrew, owned by partners Ken and Sandy Kunkel and John and Joan Grauman. Ken and John were award-winning home-brewers and, when purchasing the space, envisioned a place for making beer. Mark Hastings and Jason Shroyer, who are the brew masters and restaurant managers, opened in 2012 to make award-winning microbrews with names such as White Noise, Alpha Force and Humulus Insani.

The building that houses Überbrew was built in 1919 and "had served as the old bottling plant for the Billings Brewing Company." When they were remodeling, contractors "found a secret vault and a buried layer of glass bottles two feet thick that was probably created as they broke the bottles open during Prohibition." Sixteen bottles were in somewhat intact condition, and one bottle survived with a partially legible label.

Mike Schaer has brought life back to Montana Avenue, slowly but surely re-creating the Chicago neighborhood spirit in this once neglected area of Billings. Now it is the Billings downtown neighborhood, and perhaps someday, Montana Avenue will take on the name "Mike Schaer's Avenue."

14

CAFÉS AND BAKERIES

Where Memories Are Created and Women Meet Women

Cafés and bakeries nurtured lives in Billings, not only from the culinary delights that emerged from the kitchens and coveys but also from the conversations and community. These places were the hearths for creativity and nourishment, for they provided opportunities for starting businesses and outlets for unrelenting passions for cooking and baking. Though some of these were short-lived, others existed almost a lifetime, but mostly they changed culinary palates and patterns by bringing new flavors to Billings diners. Many provided a venue for "Where Women Meet Women," but even more, some restaurants established traditions that have remained deliciously in many memories.

In 1882, Peter Yegen and his brother Christian opened a bakery and small grocery store on Minnesota Avenue and Twenty-eighth Street selling grocery staples, canned goods and baked goods. These brothers exhibited the first entrepreneur spirits. Hubert Mohr, in 1883, added to the Vienna Bakery in the Park Hotel after purchasing the bakery from David Matheson. Here, "First-class Bread, Pies, Cakes and Rolls. Vienna and Rye Bread Fresh Every Day" were available. Jos. Parque and Co. ran the Delmonico Restaurant, "A First-Class Restaurant, open at all hours," which had a bakery associated with it. The desserts were so good that "one Richard Twohey helped himself to a pie from Joseph Parque's restaurant." The defendant was "fined $10 and costs and in default was lodged in jail." In the 1920s, Nicoll's Bakery and Confectionary satisfied the sweet tooth at 2901 First Avenue North.

First Avenue looking east at Nicoll's Bakery and Confectionery on the left, 2901 First Avenue North, 1925. *Courtesy of Billings Public Library*.

Dudleys, located in the carriage house of "the Castle." *Courtesy of Christine Twito*.

The Elmo Club on Laurel Road around 1946. *Courtesy of James M. Reich.*

In more recent history, at Dudleys Restaurant, proprietor Christine Twito believed that "living well is the best revenge." In the early 1980s, she, along with Maureen Booth, opened a small café in the Carriage House of the Castle to realize this quote. Working with Tom Nelson, Twito said, "We had the first outdoor seating. The first croissants. The first Starbucks espresso, cappuccino and iced coffee." The intimate space, located at 622 North Twenty-ninth Street, right next door to Country Cottage Antiques and the Castle Gallery and Frame Shop, was ahead of its time. Here was also the first one-dollar cup of coffee with limitless refills.

Sandwiches were sold for one dollar an inch, measured with a yardstick placed next to a French baguette from Stella's Bakery filled with marinated artichokes, Swiss and cheddar cheeses, turkey and salami slathered with grainy French mustard and drizzled with artichoke marinade. Therese Osborn baked the fresh croissants that Twito picked up daily. With no real kitchen in the café, soups such as tomato bisque, French onion and cream of asparagus were brought in, along with cheesecakes in flavors of praline and coconut.

Caterer Therese Osborn lived up to her reputation termed by Norma Buchanan as an "amazing cateress" in the 1980s and 1990s. For years, Osborn gave her culinary talents to benefit the community, including the Billings YWCA and the Yellowstone Art Museum. Originating in Egypt, she

Christine Twito and Tom Nelson relaxing after a brunch at Dudleys in the early 1980s. *Courtesy of Christine Twito.*

relocated with her oil businessman husband Chuck to Billings. Buchanan told of how Osborn learned to cook by making every recipe in the Betty Crocker cookbook. Osborn ran a successful business for many years.

Lezlie Solari and Jennie Kent started Great Beginnings, Perfect Endings, a catering company specializing in hors d'oeuvres and desserts, in the mid-1980s. They opened up Le Petite Café in the Hart-Albin Building shortly afterward. Solari's love of food began in St. Helena and Petaluma in Northern California wine country. Julia Child's cooking show mesmerized her, while her acquaintance with Robert Mondavi brought inspiration and the cooking lessons she received from Cecilia Sun Yun Chang changed her life.

After settling in Billings with her husband, Andy, she "hit it off" with Jennie Kent, who had spent time on the East Coast while her husband completed his medical residency in obstetrics and gynecology. Both Solari and Kent enrolled in classes at Le Cordon Bleu in Paris and learned French cooking techniques, with catering skills learned at Tante Marie's Cooking School in San Francisco. Out of the YWCA kitchen they rented, they made a dozen different brownies and twenty-five tortes and tarts and elaborate cakes. The cakes ranged from forest Kirsch torte and classic German chocolate cake to

Great Beginnings, Perfect Endings cake counter, 1985. *Courtesy of Lezlie Solari.*

Jennie Kent and Lezlie Solari at Great Beginnings, Perfect Endings. *Courtesy of Lezlie Solari.*

Great Beginnings
Perfect Endings

Dessert-of-the-Month

The ultimate in elegant desserts delivered throughout the coming year

"The perfect gift for someone of discriminating taste"

3-Month Plan — *$49.95*
German Cherry Almond Tart, Hazelnut Mocha Torte, Chocolate Seduction

6-Month Plan — *$99.95*
Same as 3-Month Plan, plus Lemon Cheesecake, Chocolate Rum Pecan Tart, Chocolate Strawberry Delight

9-Month Plan — *$149.95*
Same as 6-Month Plan, plus Black Forest Kirsch Torte, Chocolate Amaretto Cheesecake, Lemon Curd Tart

12-Month Plan — *$199.95*
Same as 9-Month Plan, plus Chocolate Truffles-1 pound gift box, Pina Colada Cheesecake, Amaretto Chocolate Swirl

Select the plan you wish to purchase and a certificate will be sent to the recipient announcing your gift. Months of delivery may be chosen by the recipient. Dessert-of-the-Month is truly a customized gift that continues bringing goodwill throughout the year!

2906 Grand Avenue – Phone 656-2997
Hours: 10 a.m.-6 p.m. Monday-Saturday

Delivery in Billings area only.

The Great Beginnings, Perfect Endings menu for appetizers and desserts. *Courtesy of Lezlie Solari.*

chocolate seduction. A "Dessert-of-the Month" program offered "elegant" desserts delivered throughout the year. Ray Hart approached them to cater in soups, salads, desserts and truffles to the café on the second floor of the Hart-Albin Building and scones and sweets to the Mad Hatter Tea Shoppe. The hard work involved in running the two businesses resulted in Solari selling Le Petite Café to Joanie Swords and Sandra Schiavon in 1987.

The Hart-Albin Department Store was in the Stapleton Building at the corner of First Avenue and North Broadway. Built in 1901 by the architect firm Link and Haire, this building played an important role in the development of downtown north of the tracks. While the department store anchored the first floor, the others were occupied by offices and businesses, and on the top three floors was an overnight gentlemen's club. R.M. Hart was president of the company, and B.R. Albin was secretary-treasurer and general manager. Serving all tastes and budgets, the Hart-Albin Co. sold dry goods; millinery; cloaks and suits; men's, ladies' and children's shoes; clothing; and furnishings.

After the Hart-Albin closed, Swords and Schiavon opened up Poet Street Market at 905 Poly Drive in 1990. Three years later, Cindy Prigge bought the market and for nineteen years cooked up soups, sandwiches and desserts for the Magic City. Prigge's daughter, Rachel Handley, came into the business when she was fifteen years old. With skills learned from the Scottsdale School of Culinary Arts, Handley became famous for her glazed strawberry cheesecakes, Italian cream cakes, peach scones and fresh fruit tarts. During the holidays, Poet offered a festive plum pudding with a rich buttery hard sauce. Prigge closed down the business in 2013.

The Magic City allowed for other passionate bakers and cooks to let their dreams rise. Enterprises such as Suite 753, Dancing Oven and Tipsy Cupcake provided outlets on different levels. In the mid-1990s, Sharon Weatherwax-Ripley started Suite 753 Bakery out of the basement of her home at 753 Broadwater. According to Weatherwax-Ripley, she baked wedding and birthday cakes, "thirty different breads, a full line of Danishes, croissants and muffins" to sell to wholesale outlets.

Joanie Swords started her business, Dancing Oven Bakery, so she could take her children, Harper and Madison, to work. In 2001 at 909 Fourth Street, formerly the site of Joe's Market, Swords renovated a space to bake her wedding cakes and custom desserts. Ruth Stahl purchased the bakery from Swords in 2005 to continue the cake tradition.

In 2012, Tipsy Cupcakes was one of the first businesses opened at Shiloh Crossing, the biggest strip mall development in the area, anchored by Scheels Sporting Goods. Owner Kari Jones named her shop Tipsy after her signature cupcake, pink champagne, which was also befitting of her bubbly personality. Other cupcake flavors included orange dreamsicle, salted caramel, peanut butter cup and lemon raspberry. Jones closed Tipsy Cupcake in the spring of 2015.

Favorite places for ladies to gather included Marie Halone's Level 3 Tea Room, Sweet Surrender and Cellar 301. Level 3 Tea Room served up tea and slices of quiche Lorraine from 1969 to 1983 in the Hart-Albin Company building. Sweet Surrender, a popular lunch place and a source of cakes found in a spring-colored cottage at the corner of Grand Avenue and Twenty-fourth Street West, was established in 1991 by owners Dolores Jurovich and Arleda Leedham, with Mark Smith as the manager. Here a chicken salad sandwich served on a croissant and a shrimp salad on an avocado half were popular options. Cellar 301 opened in the basement of the old chamber of commerce building in 1977. With a theme of green, colorful wallpaper and black-and-white tiled floors, it attracted many who wanted to eat there, as well as those who just wanted to view the décor. At lunch, live piano music played while diners savored the famous baked beans and ice cream pie. Jeanne Moller, who waitressed there when she was eighteen years old, remembered the frozen pie dessert being "five inches tall made with an Oreo cookie crust, coffee ice cream, whipped cream and cookie crumbles."

Morgan's Market at 1530 Twenty-fourth Street West tried to do it all aside from providing a place to gather for lunch. Fresh loaves of artisan bread emerged from the imported Italian Polin oven along with cakes, muffins and pastries. A deli supplied cheeses, meats and pâtés while gourmet food and wine offerings were available on the grocery shelves. After five years, owner Larry Handsaker and his daughter Jennifer Sullivan closed the market in 2003, selling the oven to Grand Bagel Company. Later, Arizona Bread Company moved into the space, followed by Wheat Montana Bakery and Deli.

Next to Pug Mahon's Irish Pub was the Hearth Bakery at 3005 First Avenue North. Financed by Bill "Mac" MacIntyre, the bakery's key piece of equipment was its $8,000 custom-built oven. Another $72,000 was invested in setting up the business for Paris-trained baker Sandy Dvarishkis. For a year and three months, Dvarishkis baked loaves of artisan breads including champagne, pain au levain and ciabatta. On occasion, she even sold canelés, French pastries made from egg, milk and flour baked in special copper molds. Unfortunately, the numbers did not pencil out, and the bakery closed in 2006.

Sweetgrass Sandwich Company and George Henry's also attracted a downtown business crowd at lunch. George Henry's—a former farmhouse built by Richard Crowe, a cabinetmaker from Nova Scotia, in 1896—was located at the corner of North Thirtieth Street and Fourth Avenue North. During the 1900s, the Crowe home was a boardinghouse and tearoom. Mary Ann and Andy Andrew bought the building to use as a restaurant in 1979 and named it after their fathers, George and Henry. It closed in October 2009 and was reopened in 2012 as Benson's Restaurant and

The Kit Kat Cafe, an institution at 633 Main Street since 1952. *Courtesy of the* Billings Gazette.

then Commons 1882 in 2014. During its latest reopening, Chefs Jason Corbridge of Cafe DeCamp fame and Henry Kennah of Jake's Steak House provided the stronghold in the kitchen. Bob Shinn finally retired in March 2015, after thirty-nine years of owning the oldest sandwich restaurant in Billings, the Sweetgrass Sandwich Company. The shop was known for its generous portions and rustic interior. The restaurant's name was spelled out with hundreds of white-headed nails hammered onto three boards.

Comfort food–style restaurants—Kit Kat Cafe, Stirrup Coffee Shop at the Dude Rancher Lodge and Stella's Kitchen and Bakery—warrant mentioning, for they served up hearty breakfasts and lunches. After owning the Kit Kat Cafe for twenty-seven years, Betty Miller closed the iconic restaurant days after Independence Day in 2001. Since 1952, it had been an institution at 633 Main Street. The popularity of the café even warranted a visit from President Bill Clinton in 1995 during his two-day visit when he stopped in for a cup of coffee. The Stirrup Coffee Shop at the Dude Rancher Lodge has served up breakfasts since the 1950s. St. Vincent Hospital, the Russell Refinery and Washington School contributed to the hotel built by Annabel and Percival Goan. Stella's Kitchen and Bakery began as the first

A dinner plate, soup bowl and cup from the Dude Rancher Lodge. *Courtesy of James M. Reich.*

franchise of Great Harvest Bread Company on Third and North Twenty-fourth back in the late 1970s. In 1980, Stella and Ziggy Ziegler moved to their current location at 2525 First Avenue North. The bakery became famous for its monster cakes and platter-sized cinnamon rolls at breakfast and burgers at lunch.

On January 15, 1959, the Billings Municipal Airport dining room received the name Skyview Terrace after being known as the Lorenz Airport Dining Room and the Airport Cafe in the 1940s. R.C. Whittington won the grand prize of a free round trip for two to Hawaii for winning Montana Enterprises, Inc.'s "Name-Our-Dining-Room" Contest. The name changed from the Billings Municipal Airport to Billings Logan Field in 1957, after Dick Logan, the airport manager, died. In 1971, the airport became the Billings Logan International Airport.

At Skyview Terrace, many gathered on top of the Rims "For Exotic Family Dining." Many remembered this as a special place, as the restaurant claimed, "Kiddies, you have not been forgotten. Special menus and favors for the little ones." Susan Carlson fondly retold that a scoop of ice cream in a pedestal bowl trailed streams of fog as the waitress whisked it to a table by the window. The blond girl's eyes danced with anticipation as the magical treat was set in front of her on this special day, her birthday. At the

A postcard of the Lorenz Airport Dining Room, Municipal Airport, circa 1930–45. *Courtesy of James M. Reich.*

moment the treat settled onto the table, an airplane lifted off the runway at the nearby airport. "I got dressed up. I always had to have a dress on with my hair pulled back, with black patent leather shoes." She went there for special occasions with her great-grandmother, grandparents, mom and two brothers. "My grandfather would let us order whatever we wanted to eat." Warmly, Carlson remembered "ice cream on a cloud. The ice cream was on a special metal dish with a base with a cage with holes on top of dry ice. On birthdays and anniversaries, they would do a cake for you with sparklers." Somewhere in Carlson's photograph albums was buried a Polaroid of this memorable occasion.

The dining room hosted "fashion shows with ski togs for all winter activity" and luncheons for groups such as the Federal Club and the Geologists' Wives Association. Many smorgasbords were set, with themes such as "Chuck Wagon," "Mexican," "Polynesian" and "German" serving up festive feasts. For Skyview Terrace's first anniversary, a free celebration of "hors d'oeuvres tray, champagne with each dinner, kiddie cocktails and souvenirs" was offered, along with "birthday cake compliments of the Home Bakery," with entertainment from Bob Lee and his Hammond Organ. But perhaps the most memorable food here was, as Barbara Lombardy and many others remembered, the freshly baked popovers.

These were some of the places that have come and gone that allowed "Women to Meet Women" and also for the gathering of men and children to savor and enjoy the business of life and living. The result was flavorful memories that will not be soon forgotten.

FINAL NOTES

In *Historic Restaurants of Billings*, I have provided a small sampling of the history of the food and the people who made delectable flavors in the Magic City. Unfortunately, these pages did not allow for so many other stories that have contributed to the culinary evolution of this city. But from the beginning, restaurants always provided good food and good stories.

BIBLIOGRAPHY

Baumier, Ellen. *Montana Moments: History on the Go*. N.p.: Montana Historical Society Press, 2010.

Beer Advocate. "Uberbrew." www.beeradvocate.com/community/threads/uberbrew.10043.

Biehl, Mary A. "The Granary (Billings)." *Distinctly Montana*, December 1, 2008.

Billings Daily Gazette. Advertisements. March 27, 1909; March 5, 1916.

Billings Gazette. Advertisements. February 3, 1899; February 5, 1901; June 14, 1925; June 30, 1927; February 19, 1931; May 20, 1931; April 15, 1937; November 19, 1937; March 11, 1939; January 28, 1940; February 24, 1947; July 7, 1947; July 8, 1947; July 15, 1947; August 14, 1947; September 11, 1947; September 17, 1947; September 26, 1947; October 15, 1947; October 24, 1947; December 5, 1947; January 27, 1949; May 5, 1949; July 31, 1949; October 28, 1951; February 17, 1952; July 16, 1955; May 13, 1956; February 15, 1957; June 16, 1957; May 6, 1958; January 15, 1959; March 8, 1959; June 28, 1959; September 9, 1959; September 11, 1959; October 21, 1959; October 27, 1959; October 21, 1960; May 1, 1961; May 2, 1961; February 12, 1964; April 19, 1964; December 7, 1965; July 19, 1967; April 2, 1969; June 22, 1970; April 9, 1975.

———. Announcement. March 7, 1909; March 7, 1948.

———. Announcement, "Auxillary Has Party." March 14, 1848.

———. "Billings Man Sets Good Auto Record." July 6, 1924.

———. "Birthday Party for Miss Mary Hayes." May 17, 1925.

———. "Business News: Golden Belle Plies Wiles on Midland Empire Trade." September 12, 1959.

———. "Citizens Want Rims Preserved." November 11, 1969.
———. Classified ads. March 20, 1940.
———. "Early Hostelries Play Important Role in Development of the West." November 10, 1936.
———. "8 Billings Restaurants You Will Never Eat at Again." July 6, 2014.
———. "Enterprise of the Railroad Contractors and Officials Brought into Existence." July 24, 1932.
———. "Fernandes Flew the Coop, Former Manager of Dr. Tuck Kam Leaves City." January 14, 1908.
———. "Fight in Café Leads to Fines." March 30, 1948.
———. "First Building on Billings Townsite Was Headquarters Hotel, Erected in 82." July 7, 1942.
———. "Flying Talk." September 15, 1966.
———. "Former Owners of Turf Now Operate Vegas Club." October 10, 1959.
———. "Fraternity Meet Will End Today, Helena Is Chosen for '49 Reunion." May 21, 1948.
———. "From Home to Club to Fire-Fed Ruins." January 5, 1971.
———. "Heritage Home Tour Features Architecture of City Pioneers." May 24, 2008.
———. "Kyote Class Has Banquet, Celebrates State Victory; Honors Helpers." June 4, 1924.
———. Legals. November 5, 1938.
———. Local and personal. October 26, 1907.
———. "Local Bidders Seek 3 Liquor Licenses." September 10, 1975.
———. Mary Alice Fortin Obituary. "Fortin Dies with Legacy of Giving." March 15, 2007.
———. "Musical Treat Is Provided by Two Hostesses, Mrs. O.L. Koppe and Mrs. E.O. Price Entertain." January 29 1924.
———. Northern Hotel section. July 7, 1942.
———. Notice. July 28, 1899.
———. "On Rainy Street in Montana, Nixon Window-Shops, Breakfasts, Worships: Three Hours Alone." October 10, 1960.
———. "Perfect Endings." May 22, 1985.
———. "Police Arrest Pair." July 29, 1037.
———. "Remembering the Hebgen Lake Earthquake of 1959." August 16, 2009.
———. "Retrospective: 15 Billings Restaurants You'll Never Eat at Again." January 28, 2014.

———. Review. September 17, 1976.
———. Robert J. Porter Jr. Obituary. May 7, 1993.
———. "The Secrets of Great Cheffery." October 19, 1979.
———. "Set Northern Hotel Fire Damage at $750,000 Total." September 17, 1940.
———. "Stolen Autos Are Recovered, Theft Wave Hits Billings, Red Lodge." October 27, 1956.
———. "Stubborn Turf Fire Won't Give In." August 16, 1971.
———. "Sweetgrass Sandwich Co., Longtime Local Restaurant, Closes." January 2, 2015.
———. "Yesterdays in Billings." January 18, 1967.
Billings Herald. Advertisements. June 8, 1882; December 28, 1882; April 28, 1883; May 12, 1883; August 17, 1883; September 29, 1883; October 6, 1883; November 3, 1883; November 17, 1883; June 7, 1884; September 21, 1900; July 24, 1932; September 23, 1948.
———. "Among the Roses." June 22, 1882.
———. Local news. September 21, 1882; November 23, 1882; April 14, 1883; May 5, 1883; March 29, 1884; June 28, 1884; August 9, 1884; May 2, 1885.
———. "Luzon Is Rated Oldest Cafe Here." June 17, 1948.
———. Montana news. September 14, 1882.
———. Notice. June 7, 1884; July 27, 1899.
———. Professions and business. October 26, 1882.
———. Railroad matters. March 22, 1883; June 16, 1883.
———. Town topics. September 7, 1882.
———. "Track Laying, Some Light Thrown Upon an Interesting Subject Heretofore Neglected by the Press." August 10, 1882.
Billings Petroleum Club. "BPC History." www.billingspetroleumclub.org/history.html.
Billings Senior High School Yearbook. Advertisements.
Bragg, Addison. "Bragg about Bands: A Few Steps into Memory." *Billings Gazette*, March 13, 1974.
———. "Bragg about Billings: Dining of Yesteryear Recalled." *Billings Gazette*, May 8, 2005.
———. "Right WAR, Anyway." *Billings Gazette*, June 18, 1973.
———. "Ten Feet from Starting Place." *Billings Gazette*, September 19, 1971.
Burnes, Rob. "Billings Was Rough, Then." *Billings Gazette*, January 8, 1970.
———. "Turf Case Back in Court." *Billings Gazette*, February 17, 1971.
Cioffi, Chris. "The Crowne Plaza: One Big Brick Building." *Billings Gazette*, November 22, 2014.

———. "New Restaurant Arriving in George Henry's Space." *Billings Gazette*, August 6, 2014.

Cooper, Myrtle E. *From Tent Town to City: A Chronological History of Billings, Montana 1882–1935*. N.p., 1981.

Cunningham, Lois, ed. "Old Fashion Advertising." *Full Circle: A Celebration of Billings Past and Present in Photographs*. N.p.: Schaer Publishing Company, 1995.

Deed between McCracken and Olsen and Porter. Western Heritage Center, August 31, 1945.

Falstad, Jan. "Along Schaer's Way." *Billings Gazette*, September 23, 2012.

———. "Downtown Hotel Get Another Shot at Glory When It Reopens in March." *Billings Gazette*, September 30, 2012.

———. "Great Wall Food Returns to Billings." *Billings Gazette*, February 28, 2004.

———. "Have You Heard? Jake's Twin Flourished on West End." *Billings Gazette*, August 8, 2009.

———. "Have You Heard? Thai Orchid Restaurant Closes Doors." *Billings Gazette*, October 30, 2004.

———. "Supper Club Chosen Over Franchise in the '80s." *Billings Gazette*, August 20, 2005.

———. "Vintage Supper Club Back in Business." *Billings Gazette*, October 28, 2006.

Find a Grave. "McCormick, William H. (1871–1936)." www.findagrave.com.

"Front! Goes to the Northern." *FRONT!* 4, no. 1, Western Hotels, Inc. (January–February 1960).

Geissler, Richard H. "Damage to Vegas Club Estimated at $100,000." *Billings Gazette*, December 23, 1976.

Grizzly Growler. grizzlygrowler.com. March 15, 2011.

Halone, Marie. *Level 3 & Me*. Santa Fe, NM: Likey Press, 2009.

Hardin Tribune-Herald. Special feature section. April 29, 1927.

HauntedHouses.com. "Billings Hauntings, Rex Restaurant." www.hauntedhouses.com/states/mt/rex_restaurant.htm.

———. "Dude Rancher." www.hauntedhouses.com/states/mt/dude-rancher.htm.

Hulteng, Allyn. "Khanthaly's Egg Rolls: 'First Food Truck in Montana.'" *Billings Gazette*, September 12, 2014.

Jackson Real Estate Directory. Advertisement. 1918.

Jensen, Joyce. *Pieces and Places of Billings History: Local Markers and Sites*. Billings, MT: Western Heritage Center, Artcraft Printers, 1994.

Jiusto, Chere. "Tales Spun Along the Tracks: A History of Downtown Billings." Downtown Billings Study Team. *Downtown Historic and Architectural Survey* (Fall–Winter 1998).

Johnson, Chuck, and Blanche Johnson. *Savor Montana II Cookbook: More of Montana's Finest Restaurants, Their Recipes and Their Histories*. N.p.: Wilderness Adventures Pr., 2008.

Kemmick, Ed. "Montana Ave., from Blight to Beauty in 25 Years." *Last Best News*, November 10, 2014.

Koernig, Olivia. "Billings Chop House Partners Almost Have the Table Set." *Billings Gazette*, June 16, 2007.

Kyote. Billings Senior High School yearbooks, 1955–80.

Louis, Georgeanne. "Fire Destroys Skyline Club." *Billings Gazette*, July 5, 1971.

Mercier, Laurie. "Japanese Americans in the Columbia River Basin, Historical Overview." archive.vancouver.wsu.edu/crbeha/ja/ja.htm.

Meyers, Christine. "Here Food Is Art: Unique Dining at La Toque." *Billings Gazette*, August 19, 1988.

———. "New Yorker Fell in Love with Billings." *Billings Gazette*, May 15, 2001.

National Register of Historic Places Registration Form, Application Form, Northern Hotel, United States Department of the Interior, National Park Service, OMB No. 1024-0018, Expires May 21, 2012.

Olson, Erik. "Have You Heard? Jade Palace to Close on Billings' West End." *Billings Gazette*, February 8, 2015.

———. "Have You Heard? Owners Sell Bruno's Restaurant to Start New Journey." *Billings Gazette Business*, June 14, 2015.

Polk City Directory. Advertisements, Billings, Montana. 1968, 1973.

Porter v. Porter, 473 P.2d 538 (1970). Supreme Court of Montana.

Pritchard, Matt. "Billings Brewing Co. and the Early History of Montana Craft Beer." Grizzly Growler.

Reich, James M. *Postcard History Series: Billings*. Charleston, SC: Arcadia Publishing, 2009.

Rex Hotel, National Register of Historic Places Sign Text, Yellowstone County. "Billings Historic District—Contributing Properties." montanahistorywiki.pbowrks.com.

Rightmire, Chuck, and Dick Issacson. "Early Morning Fire Destroy Elmo Club: Valued at $75,000." *Billings Gazette*, May 1, 1961.

Russell, Jeremy. "From Holling Lake to the Elmo Club, State Park Boasts a Colorful History." *Billings Gazette*, June 26, 2003.

Stevens, Karen D., and Dee Ann Redman. *Billings A to Z*. N.p.: Friends of the Library, 2000.

BIBLIOGRAPHY

United States Department of Interior, National Park Service/National Register of Historic Places Registration Form, Northern Hotel, Yellowstone County, MT, OMB No. 1024-0018, Expires 5/21/2012.

Webb, Jaci. "Meet the Chef: Stella Ziegler at Stella's Kitchen and Bakery." *Billings Gazette*, June 22, 2012.

———. "Weekly Webb: Painting a Way of Life." *Billings Gazette*, March 7, 2014.

Weekly Times. Local layout. August 16, 1894.

Weirather, Linda. "Research on the Northern Hotel." Courtesy of the Western Heritage Center.

Western News. Montana items. September 4, 1907.

West High School Yearbook. Advertisements.

Westward. Billings West High School yearbooks, 1962–80.

Windmill. windmillrestaurant.net/history.php.

INDEX

INDEX

M

N

Y

Z

ABOUT THE AUTHOR

Photo by Tony Smith.

Stella Fong writes, cooks and plays in Billings, Montana. For sixteen years, she has called Montana's Trailhead (once also known as the Magic City) home after relocating from San Diego, California. Fong shares her love of food and adventure through her contributions to *Yellowstone Valley Woman Magazine*, *Big Sky Journal*, *Blue Water Sailing*, *Western Art and Architecture* and *Magic Magazine*. Online, her blog postings and stories can be found at thelastbestplates.com, lastbestnews.com, vinography.com and stellafong.com. Her articles have also appeared in *Cooking Light*, *Fine Cooking* and the *Washington Post*. Through her food and wine classes she teaches for the Montana State University–Billings Foundation, she continues to bring flavor and knowledge. For years, she taught cooking classes for Sur La Table, Williams Sonoma, Gelson's Super Market, Macy's Cellars and Great News! Cooking School.

Visit us at
www.historypress.net

This title is also available as an e-book